Sophie Grigson is a cook, food writer and television presenter with over 20 books to her name and nine television series for BBC, Channel 4 and UKTV Food. She has also written columns and articles for the *Evening Standard, Independent, Sunday Times, Country Living, BBC Good Food* and *Waitrose Food Illustrated.* During this time she has been raising her children, running her cookery school in Oxford and presenting television shows for The Travel Channel. On impulse, after interviewing Russell Norman about his book, *Venice,* in 2019 she sold or gave away the majority of her belongings and packed herself into her small car to move to Puglia in the south of Italy.

Also by Sophie Grigson:

Food for Friends
Sophie Grigson Eat Your Greens
Sophie Grigson's Ingredients Book
Sophie Grigson's Meat Course
Sophie Grigson's Taste of the Times
Sophie Grigson Cooks Vegetables
Fish
Sophie's Table
Sophie Grigson's Herbs
Sophie Grigson's Feasts for a Fiver
Sophie Grigson's Sunshine Food
Organic
The Complete Sophie Grigson Cookbook
The First-Time Cook
Sophie Grigson's Country Kitchen
Vegetables
The Soup Book
Spices

A CURIOUS ABSENCE OF CHICKENS

A journal of life, food and recipes
from Puglia

SOPHIE GRIGSON

First published in 2021
by Headline Home
an imprint of Headline Publishing Group

1

Cataloguing in Publication Data is available from the British Library

ISBN 978 1 4722 7886 9
eISBN 978 1 4722 7887 6

Headline's policy is to use papers that are natural, renewable and recyclable products and made from wood grown in sustainable forests. The logging and manufacturing processes are expected to conform to the environmental regulations of the country of origin.

Publishing Director: Lindsey Evans
Senior Editor: Kate Miles
Copy Editor: Annie Lee
Proofreaders: Anne Sheasby and Jill Cole
Indexer: Caroline Wilding

HEADLINE PUBLISHING GROUP
An Hachette UK Company
Carmelite House
50 Victoria Embankment
London EC4Y 0DZ

www.headline.co.uk
www.hachette.co.uk

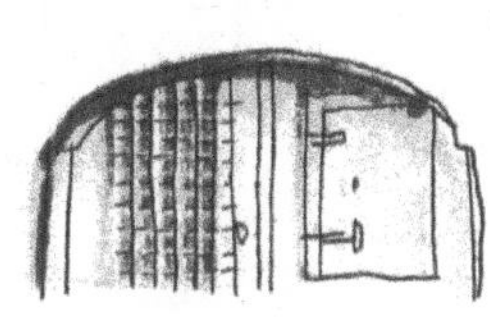

For the Ceglie Pods, who have shared their enthusiasm for Puglia, food, wine, good company, humour, life and wisdom so freely.
Grazie, cari amici.

CONTENTS

Introduction 1

Cooks' notes 8

About the recipes 8

1 Saturday is Market Day 11

2 (Almost) the Noisiest Place in Town 55

3 Five Hundred Miles of Seaside 81

4 Wood-fired Ovens 115

5 The Elixir of Life 143

6 The Stuff of Life 159

7 But Where are All the Cows? 193

8 Sustenance for Summer Nights 215

9 La Mia Campagna – Tales from the Orchard 239

10 Almonds are Not the Only Nut (but you might be forgiven for thinking they were) 275

Acknowledgements 301

Index 303

Conversion Charts 310

INTRODUCTION

After an absence of nearly forty years, I arrived back in Puglia on 10 May 2019, me and my purple aubergine of a car, rammed full with pretty much everything I owned. We entered by a back route, unpropitious with its potholes and twists and turns, squiggling along the northern perimeter of the Gargano Peninsula to Vieste at its tip. Here at last.

About a year earlier I'd had one of those light-bulb moments. I would move lock, stock and barrel to the south of Italy. I'd just interviewed the author and restaurateur Russell Norman about his book *Venice*, an account of a year lived in the backstreets of Venice learning to cook like the locals. There was an audience, so I was trying to appear professional and thoughtful, but was horribly distracted by two thoughts: (1) This man is so bloody gorgeous and charming, and (2) I am so jealous – why haven't I ever done something like this? Two days later, I was procrastinating my way down an internet path to nowhere when I came across a story about a little town called Candela in the north of Puglia that was paying people to move there. And right then and there it struck me. I could and I would. I was going to move to the south of Italy. After eleven months of sorting, clearing, organising, saying goodbyes, my Oxford flat was empty and my car was so full I could barely squeeze myself in. I dropped the keys through the letterbox and headed south.

Vieste soon squashed any lingering doubts that I was doing the right thing. Like so many of the beautiful white hill towns of Puglia, the heart is the medieval *centro storico*, with winding streets and stairways, alleys and arches, and a greater or lesser number of tourist shops and restaurants. So it began, with a meal in a restaurant picked at random, where the chef/patron/brothers had a yen for molecular playfulness, bracketed with the traditional in the form of tiny octopuses braised in tomato and red wine. And later an epic firework display over the harbour, perfectly framed by my bedroom window, to welcome me back. It also happened to be the *festa* of the town's patron saint. Coincidence. Surely.

Candela itself turned out to be a fetching little white hill village, close to the Bari–Naples motorway, but otherwise in the middle of nowhere. Its one claim to fame is La Trasonna, Italy's narrowest street, just 35cm wide. As streets go, it's also very, very short. At the mayor's office I discovered that the money was long gone, but by then I'd realised that it wasn't the place for me. I needed to be further south, somewhere I could earn a living with my minimal Italian. I set off again, on the hunt for a home.

After a few weeks of moseying around mostly in unseasonable torrents of rain, the small town of Ceglie Messapica found me. It's in the verdant, *trulli*-strewn Itria Valley, near the better-known Ostuni. The outskirts are ugly, which is true of most Italian towns, but the centre is pretty and unassuming. There are no particular tourist attractions, but the town styles itself as a *città gastronomica*. In practice this means that there are a lot of restaurants, most of them good and a handful that are excellent. There is also a professional cookery school for young chefs, set around a frescoed courtyard in the very heart of the old town. A stroke of luck leads me to a small sunlit house with stupidly steep stairs and pale ochre and ivory stone walls. I know immediately that this is home.

And I thought I knew a bit about Italian cooking . . . Discovering how Puglia eats

Though Puglian cooking is obviously Italian, it has a beating heart that is all its own. It takes, ooh, about all of twenty-four hours to begin to spot the differences. Keep looking and they merge into a unique cuisine carved out of the land, poverty, cavalcades of invaders and a joyful greed for good food.

You soon learn here that food is highly localised, and universally treasured. In my new home town, I asked for a '*pasticciotto*' (a divinely crumbly pastry filled with crème patissière). Oh, mad Englishwoman! 'They're a speciality of Lecce (all of forty miles away). We don't make them here.' Actually you can get them all over the place (including the deep-freeze section of a local supermarket), but her point was clear.

Ten miles in the other direction is the town of Cisternino, where so many of the town's restaurants aren't restaurants, at least not in the daytime. They're butchers shops, selling impeccably displayed raw meat to whoever wants it. The display is still there in the evening, but the back rooms have opened and the butchery is transformed into a *braceria* or *rosticceria.* Hell for vegans, paradise for carnivores. Charcoal-grilled steaks, sausages and chops, but best of all, to my mind, are the *bombette,* little rolls of meat and cheese and herbs, oozing and tender.

In Oria, I am introduced to the *pignata,* a clay pot for cooking stews, buried overnight in the embers of a wood-fired oven. Here they stew beef, pork, horse or donkey in a lake of rich tomato sauce. Some of that sauce is siphoned off to dress pasta, the rest eaten with the now phenomenally tender meat. Over on the coastal instep, in pre-season Porto Cesareo, I order a *pignata di polpo.* Octopus cooked so slowly in its earthenware that it is as soft as butter, richly seasoned, but with barely a trace of sauce.

When I first looked out from the heights of Candela's main street, the early June landscape was a patchwork of golden wheat stubble, olive groves, vines jacketed in plastic sheeting to protect against storms, and wind turbines. Hundreds of wind turbines, harvesting the gusts of air. There it was, spread out below me – wheat, wine and olive oil. The foundation stones of every meal in this blessed, endlessly fought-over (Ostrogoths, Greeks, Normans, Arabs, Austrians, Turks, French, Spaniards and Romans have all claimed it at one time or another), now often-overlooked patch of land.

Add to that the sweet, sweet tomatoes, the bitter *lampascioni* (muscari bulbs), garlic, rich cheeses (especially burrata, created here in Puglia a century ago), cured *capocollo* and chilli-seared *soppressata* salami. Only an hour's drive away, east and west, the long coastline delivers fish, octopus, crabs and mussels to strings of small ports with their bobbing fishing boats and early-morning harbour markets. One of Candela's home products is *grano arso*, literally burnt grain, not the mistranslated 'big bottom' that makes me giggle childishly. Whole grains of wheat are roasted to within a millimetre of their lives, then ground to a fine flour and used for pasta (particularly *orecchiette*) and bread. Negroamaro and Primitivo grapes put flasks of wine on tables and in the increasing warmth of the June sun, the inhabitants of Turi turn out to celebrate the Sagra della Ciliegia Ferrovia, the Festival of the Railway Cherry, a plump, juicy variety named for the train tracks that ran alongside the original grand-daddy of a tree.

I knew when I arrived that Puglia was a region I wanted to get to know intimately, to understand the culture, life, history and geography, reflected through the prism of the food that's put on the tables of locals and of tourists, too. I'm reminded of my twenty-year-old self, scribbling in notebooks as I first travelled through Italy's south, only this time I'm back to stay.

Covid, before, during and hopefully after

When I moved into my little house on 6 June 2019, the words coronavirus and pandemic meant little to me or most of Ceglie Messapica's inhabitants. The word Covid did not exist. The world had no idea of what was to come.

That first summer was wonderful. It seemed that I had arrived in a town that lived life to the full, with events and celebrations of one sort or another every weekend and often midweek, too. It's a party town, I told friends back in the UK. Gradually I made new friends, I tootled off on little trips to other parts of Puglia, I sampled new foods and drinks and generally had a ball. Autumn and winter were quieter but the restaurants were still full every weekend.

Then Covid-19 happened and the party ended as spring set in. 2020's first lockdown brought silent streets and muted the natural Italian exuberance that comes with warmer weather. The exploratory excursions I had planned to the very south and the very north of Puglia were now impossible. Still, compared to many we've been lucky here. The cases of Covid in the town remain low and food supplies were never an issue.

Much of what I write about in this book is based on my experiences before Covid, but it also spans spring to autumn of 2020. It's been a strange time to move to a new country and a strange time to be writing a book about food. By the time it is published in early summer 2021 we will have a new president in the White House and new vaccines to keep us safe. Ceglie Messapica, Puglia, the world will be finally trundling along the path to recovery and renewal. New horizons and new hope are ahead of us all.

Cooks' notes

All spoon measurements are rounded unless otherwise specified. I use a conventional 15ml tablespoon, 10ml dessertspoon and 5ml teaspoon. Eggs are free-range and large, unless stated otherwise. Treat all cooking times as guidelines, not hard rules. Terms like 'bunch' and 'handful' are deliberately vague, requiring the cook to interpret to their own taste and according to availability. If in doubt, use herbs generously. Parsley is always flat-leaf and fresh, as is mint. Basil is always, always fresh. Oregano is dried. Bay leaves are fine either way, fresh or dried. Olive oil, of course, is always extra virgin. Use lots of it.

About the recipes

Most of the recipes in *A Curious Absence of Chickens* are traditional Puglian dishes. A few have been tweaked here and there to make them easier to cook away from their home territory, or because I liked them better with my variations melded in. For interest and as a lure to bring you readers to this blessed land, I've included a handful of dishes that can only be cooked in Puglia because this is the only place you will find the essential ingredients, such as the *olive dolci*, sweet olives. Finally, I couldn't resist slipping in a scattering of interlopers, recipes that I love and that seem to me to fit beautifully within the Puglian context, like my mother's sweetmeat cake recipe.

Beeswax cloths

It took me a while, but I now love my beeswax cloths (or wraps, if you prefer) and use them all the time. They don't completely replace clingfilm, but they do reduce the amount you get through, which is a good thing. They also reduce the number of times when you struggle to find the edge of the clingfilm (see note on page 10) and swear as it rips midway, or as you cut your finger on the serrated metal strip. This is also a good thing.

You can buy beeswax cloths readymade, but they're expensive, even if they do last for 6–12 months. They are often too small, as well. Luckily it's easy enough to make them yourself, and you can cut them to the size that suits you. You may be able to buy beeswax from local beekeepers, otherwise look online. There are plenty of instructions and much in-depth information to be found on the internet, but briefly, this is the way that I make my beeswax cloths:

For one 30cm square of cotton or linen cloth (old bed linen works nicely), grate 20g of beeswax and toss lightly with 1 teaspoon of olive oil. Line a large baking tray with baking parchment and preheat the oven to 140°C/120°C fan/gas 1. Lay out the square of cloth on the baking tray and scatter the wax and oil mixture over it. Melt in the oven for 4–6 minutes. Using either a silicone brush, or a small clean sponge, brush the melted wax around the cloth, making sure that it is totally covered, with the wax reaching right to the edges. Pick the cloth up with tongs and gently waft it around for a few minutes until cool. All done.

Cleaning up: Don't wash the waxy grater and tongs directly in the sink or dishwasher. The wax will clog the drains. Instead, put a heatproof bowl into the sink and pour boiling water over the utensils and into the bowl, to remove the residue. Then wash as normal. Let the bowl of water cool down and pop it into the fridge for an hour or two. The wax will rise and set in a thin film over the water. Lift it off and discard.

Using and cleaning your beeswax cloths:
Use the warmth of your hands to mould the cloths around whatever it is you want to wrap – a bowl, a plate, a sandwich,

a piece of cake. Do not use them to wrap raw chicken, meat or fish.

Clean them in cold water with a dab of washing-up liquid, then leave to dry. Store in a kitchen drawer or cupboard away from heat.

Note

. . . If you want your clingfilm hell to disappear completely, store it in the fridge. The box may go a bit soggy, but the clingfilm unrolls without a hitch. Thank you, lovely Sally, who introduced me to this genius tip in her Puglian kitchen.

1

SATURDAY IS MARKET DAY

Our market is unremarkable. It is small compared to the Saturday market in nearby Ostuni or the Wednesday market in Martina Franca, but it's the one I go to almost every week. It's the ritual and the now-familiar faces I enjoy as much as the content. My ritual begins with the ten-minute stroll down the Corso Verdi, right along via Francesco Argentieri, turning off just after the *farmacia* into via Cesare Beccaria which leads me straight down into the genteel hubbub of market day. It ends with coffee in Alter Gusto, the fanciest *pasticceria* in town (it has a flowing molten chocolate wall, no less), bags of shopping at my ankles, essential fortification before the tramp back up the hill.

In between there are fruit and vegetable stalls, knickers and trainers, plastic bowls and metal pasta rods. Down in the small, un-picturesque piazza at the back there are a couple of vans selling fresh fish from the coast, others with cheeses and salami, and the small stalls of very local growers with their own small heaps of abundance from their small vegetable patches and small orchards. If they are lucky, they sell out early, leaving plenty of time for a coffee hooched up with a shot of cheap grappa.

The quality of the fruit and vegetables is, of course, impeccable. Each season brings its particular staples, piled up in swiftly diminishing and swiftly replenished mounds. Crates of whatever is at its peak of production are borne off by hard-bargaining housewives, ready to preserve for the next year until the season comes around again.

In March 2020, the abrupt disappearance of the market, mid-artichoke season, seemed one of the most shocking symptoms of the lockdown itself. Two months later, the first nervous return of a handful of food stalls, protected by police wielding temperature guns and doling out hand-sanitiser, heralded the possibility that we might learn to live with the damnable Covid.

Queer gear

Back in the day, the wholesale fruit and veg sellers of London's New Covent Garden Market used to call exotic and unusual fruit and veg 'queer gear'. I visited occasionally, back in the 80s and 90s when I lived in London, and I think it is fair to say that the vendors were not modern reconstructed men. The women who worked among them had a lot to put up with. Are they more woke now? Maybe. These days, when I type 'queer gear' into Google, up leaps 'rubber wear experience'. Hmmm.

Anyway, the point is that Puglia has its own selection of queer gear of the vegetable variety. On market stalls, at the *fruttivendolo* (a favourite word of mine, it means greengrocer) or in the supermarket there are always mini-mountains of round or oval green vegetables that look something like a deflated melon or a pumped-up cucumber. *Caroselli* and *baratelli* or *barattiere* are indeed all balanced somewhere between cucumber and melon. They are eaten peeled and cut into wedges or discs on a daily basis, as an accompaniment to pasta. Something green and fresh and crunchy to lighten the full-on carbyness of the midday meal.

Summer brings bunches of serpent beans, *fagiolini serpente*, almost as long as my forearm. Every time I buy them, my main man at the market reminds me to cook them with spaghetti. Dutifully, I do. They go into the pan of boiling spaghetti about halfway through the cooking time, roughly half as much snake as pasta. Dressed with garlic, anchovy, a little chilli and a handful of halved cherry tomatoes fried swiftly in lots of olive oil, they turn out most pleasingly.

The inhabitants of Puglia were once sneeringly known as *mangiafoglie*, leaf-eaters, and it's true, they do have a passion for green leafy vegetables. There are crates and crates of greens in the market, most of them blessed with the hint of bitterness that the Pugliese love so much. Among them I can now recognise the following: *puntarelle*, which are, I think, the larger leaves of *cicoria* which is not at all the same as chicory; *cicoria*, or *cicoriella*, sports thick hollow stems and leaves and comes in colossal bunches. It's sometimes known as *catalogna*, which may or may not denote a particular varietal difference. It is a classic accompaniment to *fave*, purééd dried broad beans. *Cicoria da campo* are dandelion leaves. *Cime di rapa*, usually translated as turnip tops, is the darling of the greens, consumed in massive quantity with pasta. Otherwise they are all usually served boiled, then dressed with lemon juice and olive oil, possibly with a little garlic or chilli or tomato.

Agretti or *barba di frate* (monk's beard) gets much the same treatment. It looks like a shock of green hair and you would be forgiven for thinking it was related to oniony chives. It's actually a salt-loving plant that grows easily in coastal areas. Tastewise it's pleasant, with a teensy hint of saline and iodine, but really not that exciting. I like it in a frittata (see page 47). If you set fire to *agretti* you end up with soda ash, which was one of the essential components used by the medieval glassblowers of Murano.

Colder weather also heralds the arrival of *lampascioni* or

lampagioni. They lurk, muddy and brown and tangled, on the market stalls. The uninitiated might guess that they were some sort of shallot or pickling onion but they would be wrong. *Lampascioni* are the bulbs of the tassel hyacinth or muscari, closely related to springtime blue grape hyacinths. They have a natural mild bitterness, which of course makes them another Puglian favourite. They are cooked in every which way, pickled, fried, boiled, baked, in stews and frittatas and with pasta.

The cult of the cherry tomato

Tomatoes are, of course, delicious and plentiful in the south of Italy. That's hardly a surprise. What has surprised me is discovering that the cooking tomato of choice is the cherry tomato, particularly in summer dishes. For salads, the top summer tomato is larger but still a little green and crisp. Large fully ripe red tomatoes, the sort I'd choose for a salad, are regarded as being only good for *sugo*, tomato sauce and other slow-cooked cold-weather dishes.

Traditionally, the family would gather together midsummer, surrounded by crates of ripe red *sugo* tomatoes, working together to chop and cook down cauldrons of tomato sauce. Puréed and sieved, it was bottled and laid down for the autumn and winter when the tomato season was long gone. A few still do this, but these days tomatoes of all types are available all year round, from the market as well as the supermarket. Most people will be buying fresh, tinned or bottled passata with scant regard for tradition or seasonality.

Towards the end of July *ramasole* of *pomodori appesi*, skeins of Regina tomatoes, a little larger than a cherry tomato but still small, make their unmistakable annual debut. They hang from nails against white walls in beautiful red bunches, like outsized scarlet grapes. There they stay for months, gradually shedding some of their newly harvested red as they age into a rich burnt orange. Remarkably they stay plump and good right through the winter, thanks to their tough skin.

Back to those cherry tomatoes. They are treated with an insouciant reverence here, beloved for the deep, sweet-sharp umami they bring to so many simple dishes. I've learnt not to throw them into a pan in quantity but to use them almost as a seasoning, added sparingly to impart a subtler subtext that swings harmoniously with the aromas of olive oil, garlic and parsley. So, don't be surprised, as I was, when a recipe for four people calls for just 8 or 12 cherry tomatoes, and don't ramp up the quantity. The idea here is not to swamp the flavour of other ingredients, but to accent and enhance. It works.

Herbs

Parsley, parsley, parsley, basil and mint in the summer; parsley, parsley, parsley, dried oregano, sage and rosemary in the winter. That's about it. Flat-leaf parsley finds its way into almost every savoury dish ever made here. When you buy fruit or vegetables from the market or greengrocer, a handful of perfectly fresh, vibrant parsley is thrown in for free. Very civilised.

It's impossible to get coriander leaf or dill unless you grow them yourself. Wild fennel, which grows everywhere, is my dill substitute. Not the same, but close enough for most purposes.

Chillies

I have no intention of ever getting married again, but just supposing I did in some parallel universe, I'd replace the traditional bouquet of roses or lilies with a bouquet of Puglian chillies straight from the market. Sold in handsome bunches, they are as pretty as a picture, glossy, red and full of vigour against the dark green of their stems.

Cute they may be, but they pack a powerful punch. They lie somewhere between your average serrano chilli, the common or garden variety sold in most British supermarkets, and the fearsome Scotch bonnet. They are widely used in Puglia, but with moderate restraint. A pleasing tingle is all that is required. Those who want more heat will simply slice a raw chilli straight into their pasta at the table.

All the recipes in this book are calibrated to work with serrano chillies. If you do have proper Puglian chillies you may want to reduce quantities a little.

Capers

Caper plants are easily pleased. They like nothing better than rocks and crevices and hot salty air. Give them a craggy cliff or a dry-stone wall, a boulder-strewn field or harbour cobbles and they will make it their home, threading fine roots down through invisible gaps to find some impossible sustenance.

You are never far from a caper plant here and that means that capers, the flower buds, are free for the taking if you can be bothered to pick them. It takes patience to pick enough to see a family through the year, but once you've done that the rest is easy. Naturally that means that capers feature boldly in local cooking.

Last summer Sid, my son, and I salted our own capers for the first time. Just one jar of them as we are not gifted with massive patience, especially when it's a broiling 35°C outside. The preserving process is straightforward enough. First you soak the capers in cold water for 2 days or so, changing the water twice a day. Next you layer them with lots of salt in an airtight container for a few more days, giving them a gentle shake every now and then. Soon they develop their characteristic white spots. Then it's a quick rinse and into clean jars together with a mix of half-and-half wine vinegar and water to finish the job. A week later they are ready to go.

Our capers were excellent, though I say it myself, but soon we'd eaten every last one of them. Back to the market again, where I bought a huge jar of capers, picked and pickled by somebody's uncle. Enough, I hope, to last me through to next year's caper days.

Caponata

I included a recipe for Sicilian *caponata* in my second book, published in the early 90s. I still use the same recipe and I adore it just as much as I did then. It's an unexpectedly brilliant sweet and sour blend of aubergine, celery, capers, olives and tomato that works magic as part of an antipasto, or as a spirited side dish or in sandwiches. It never fails, even with people who are convinced they loathe aubergines or celery.

Now, thirty years later, I discover that *caponata* is a collective noun, not a singular one. There are any number of different *caponatas* in Sicily – fish *caponata,* cauliflower *caponata,* squash *caponata,* courgette *caponata* and many more – and I also discover that Puglia has its own *caponata,* which is more of a mixed vegetable stew, including aubergine and tomato and some combination of peppers, carrots, courgettes and presumably whichever other vegetables are available.

At this point I would like to apologise to the chef and staff of the Oxford restaurant where I complained that their *caponata* was not a *caponata* at all. To be fair it did lack the sweet-sour element, but for all I know it may have been based on somebody's Pugliese or Sicilian *nonna*'s special, entirely authentic version. Mind you, it still didn't taste as good as my original recipe.

My Old Recipe for Caponata

Sweet-sour Aubergine with Tomato, Olives and Capers

Best served at room temperature, even better the day after it has been made. Salting the aubergine is not 100% necessary, but it does pull out the mildly metallic undertones, and it certainly reduces the amount of oil they absorb when frying.

Green olives are more traditional but I prefer black ones for *caponata*.

Serves 4–6

1 large aubergine, diced
salt and freshly ground black pepper
6 tablespoons extra virgin olive oil
6 stems of celery, thinly sliced
1 onion, chopped
1 x 400g tin of chopped tomatoes or 450g fresh tomatoes, skinned and chopped
2 tablespoons caster sugar
4 tablespoons red wine vinegar
1 teaspoon grated nutmeg
1 heaped teaspoon capers, rinsed if salted
12 green or black olives, stoned and sliced
2 tablespoons chopped flat-leaf parsley, plus a little extra, roughly chopped, for serving

Spread out the aubergine dice in a colander, sprinkle with salt and set aside for ½–1 hour. Press gently to extract as much water as possible. Dry on kitchen paper or a clean tea towel.

Heat 4 tablespoons of the olive oil in a heavy-based frying pan. Sauté the celery until browned (and I mean properly browned). Scoop out and set aside. Fry the aubergine in the same oil until browned and tender, adding a little extra oil if necessary. Scoop out and leave to cool.

Add the remaining oil to the pan and fry the onions gently until golden. Add the tomatoes and simmer for 10 minutes or so, until thick and pulpy. Next add the sugar, vinegar and nutmeg and cook for a further 5–10 minutes, until you have a rich sweet-and-sour sauce. Add a little salt and plenty of freshly ground black pepper. Stir in the capers, olives, parsley, aubergine and celery. Taste and adjust the seasoning – the flavours will soften as the *caponata* cools. Serve with a sprinkling of chopped parsley.

NB: If you want to make double, treble or more, toss the aubergine in olive oil and the celery in olive oil, spread out in separate baking trays and roast at around 200°C/180°C fan/ gas 6 for 20–30 minutes, stirring once or twice, until browned and tender. Make the tomato base and continue as above.

Caponata di Zucca Rossa

Squash Caponata with Raisins and Toasted Almonds

By late September huge winter squashes arrive in the market and shops. *Zucca rossa* is the general term for orange-fleshed squashes. The prevalent variety here is a beautiful pumpkin-sized squash, voluptuously curvaceous with a soft satin sheen to its bronzed orange rind. It's not as sweet as a butternut squash but otherwise tastes similar.

Like aubergine *caponata,* this one is best eaten at room temperature.

Serves 6

600g butternut squash or other orange-fleshed winter squash
4 stems of celery, trimmed and thinly sliced
5 tablespoons extra virgin olive oil
1 onion, chopped
1 x 400g tin of chopped tomatoes
salt and freshly ground black pepper
2 tablespoons caster sugar
4 tablespoons red wine vinegar
1 teaspoon ground cinnamon
3 tablespoons chopped flat-leaf parsley
45g flaked almonds, toasted
40g raisins
2 tablespoons capers, rinsed if salted
100g black olives, stoned and sliced
a small handful of mint leaves, roughly chopped

De-rind the squash and remove and discard the seeds. Cut into 2cm cubes. You will need around 500g prepared weight. Slice the celery stems into half-moons, about as thick as a 1 euro coin. Line a baking tray with a couple of layers of kitchen paper.

Now to the first cooking stage – you must cook the squash and celery separately, either one after the other in the same pan (more time, less washing up) or get two roomy pans heating on the stove at once. Add a couple of tablespoons of olive oil to each one. Once it is hot, add the squash to one pan, the celery to the other. Sauté over a lively heat, until both are browned. It takes a surprisingly long time for celery to brown because of all that water trapped in its cells, which has to evaporate off before browning can begin. The squash needs to be just cooked through, but hopefully not collapsing. Tip each one out on to the paper-lined tray to drain off some of the oil, but try to leave a little oil in one of the frying pans.

Put the oily pan back on the heat, lower this time, and fry the onions in it slowly, adding a little more oil if needed, until they are soft and very tender. Add the chopped tinned tomatoes and a small glass of water. Season with salt and plenty of freshly ground black pepper. Simmer gently for 20 minutes or so, until thick. Stir in the sugar, vinegar and cinnamon and simmer for another 2–3 minutes. Set aside a little of the parsley and the almonds for garnishing and stir the rest into the sauce, along with the squash and celery, the raisins, capers and olives. Give it all a final couple of minutes over the heat to bring all those flavours together, then leave to cool until tepid. Taste and adjust the seasoning (you'll probably need more salt to balance the sweetness of the squash and sugar). Serve at room temperature, sprinkled with the reserved parsley and almonds, and the mint.

Frittele di Fiori di Zucchina Ripiene

Courgette Flower Fritters with Ricotta, Lemon and Pistachios

I've tried doing all sorts of things with courgette flowers, like adding them to a risotto or a soup, or even a salad, but honestly all they contribute is a splash of yellow. The whole raison d'être of the courgette flower, foodwise, is that it makes an utterly delightful fritter. Nothing more, nothing less.

Given that they have a delicate flavour, the best batter has to be a light veil of tempura made at the last minute with icy cold water. The chill of the water is important as it reduces the development of gluten in the batter, which makes it much crisper.

Stuffing the courgette flowers is optional. I used to think it ridiculously fiddly until I discovered the magic of piping bags. Now I fill courgette flowers at the drop of a hat and feel mighty smug. Given that (a) courgette flowers tear easily, (b) life is too short, and (c) they taste fine, there is absolutely no need to remove the stamen/pistil inside each flower. Don't chuck out the stems, either. Battered and fried, they are almost as good as the flowers themselves.

Serves 4 as a starter

12 courgette flowers
extra flour, for dusting
sunflower oil, for deep-frying
lemon wedges

For the filling
150g ricotta
finely grated zest of 1 lemon (reserve the lemon to serve)
20g roughly chopped pistachios
salt and lots of freshly ground black pepper
a splash of milk if required

For the batter
1 egg yolk
100g plain flour
½ teaspoon salt
200ml iced water

Rinse the courgette flowers under the cold tap, then wrap loosely in kitchen paper and stash in an airtight container or plastic bag in the fridge until needed. They'll remain usable for 2–3 days.

To make the filling, mix the ricotta with the lemon zest, pistachios, salt and pepper. It should be creamy and moist. If it looks dry, add a small splash or two of milk. Pile the mixture into a piping bag and knot loosely. Keep in the fridge until about half an hour before you intend to fry your courgette flowers. Take out and allow it to come back to room temperature or thereabouts.

Snip off the end of the piping bag. One by one, tease open your courgette flowers and fill with the ricotta mixture, carefully folding the petals back over the filling to cover completely. Gently twist the ends together.

Cut the zested lemon into wedges and set aside for serving. Line a tray or plate with a double layer of kitchen paper. Put 3 or 4 tablespoons of flour (for dusting) on to another plate. Put your oil on to heat. Now make the tempura batter. Put the egg yolk into a bowl, add the flour and salt, and mix in the water, which needs to be ultra-cold. Do this swiftly and don't worry about little lumps of flour in the batter.

Quickly set up your production line on the work surface beside the hob. Closest to the hot oil, put the tempura batter, next to that the plate of flour, and next to that your stuffed courgette flowers. Put the kitchen-paper-lined plate close to the hot oil, either on the other side of the hob, or just behind the batter, whichever works better for you.

Now take the courgette flowers a couple at a time, turn them in the flour so that they are lightly coated, then dip them into the batter, shake off the excess and lay them in the hot oil. Fry for around 4 minutes, turning occasionally, until the batter is crisp and just lightly browned at the tips. Scoop out with a slotted spoon and lay on the kitchen paper to drain briefly. Fry the remaining courgette flowers in the same way. Sprinkle lightly with salt and serve with the lemon wedges for those that want them.

Peppers and *peperonata*

Red, yellow and green peppers are available all year round here, just as they are practically everywhere else. What distinguishes them are their twisting contorted bodies, frequently blending bright colour and dark green in a single fruit. Despite this they still manage to come into their own in the summer, when their glossy plumpness and caressable curves make them the starlets of any stall. And the summer heat deepens the sweetness and flavour while abundance batters down the price. Every third or fourth person at the market is bearing a crate or two of *peperoni*, taking them home to grill, to stew, to roast, to stuff, and above all to preserve for a winter night.

Here in Puglia, every town seems to have its own particular way of preserving peppers. They are, by and large, variants of the same thing. The ingredient lists will include, besides the peppers themselves, extra virgin olive oil (of course), garlic, fresh, dried or ground *peperoncini* (chillies), salt and some or all or none of the following: celery, tomatoes, capers, mint, basil, oregano.

Like the relishes themselves, the familiar names vary from one town to another. Downstairs Maria (born here, but brought up in Taranto) makes *pipone* (see page 154), while the inhabitants of Martina Franca, all of eleven miles away, make *plic e plac*, very similar but with a little tomato added for acidity and sauciness.

Another name, *peperonata*, is recognised across the region, but had me mightily confused, as I've always thought of it as a freshly cooked side dish. Further reading and scouting and I now understand that here in Puglia, and possibly throughout Italy, *peperonata* just refers to any delicious mess of cooked peppers. Eat it now, eat it in 6 months' time, tomatoes or no tomatoes, onions or no onions, capers or no capers, it's still *peperonata*.

Peperonata di Sophie

Sautéd Mess of Peppers

Delicious hot, warm or at room temperature, with a roast chicken or steak, or piled on bruschetta with scoops of fresh ricotta and sprigs of basil.

Serves 4–6

1 onion, sliced
4 tablespoons extra virgin olive oil
4 red peppers, deseeded and cut into long strips
3 cloves of garlic, crushed
½ teaspoon fennel seeds
¼ teaspoon dried chilli flakes
500g tomatoes, skinned and roughly chopped (or 1 x 400g tin of chopped tomatoes)
2 tablespoons tomato purée
1 teaspoon sugar (unless your tomatoes are exceptionally good)
salt and freshly ground black pepper

Sauté the onion in the olive oil until lightly coloured. Add the peppers, garlic, fennel seeds and chilli flakes and cook for a further couple of minutes. Cover the pan and let them cook down gently in their own juices for 5 minutes. Now add the remaining ingredients and 200ml of water, bring to the boil, then simmer gently for half an hour, uncovered, stirring occasionally. Taste and adjust the seasoning.

Peperoni alla Mollica

Puglian Fried Peppers with Breadcrumbs and Capers

Crisp fried breadcrumbs, soft sweet fried peppers, a waft of mintiness – altogether a great combination. Serve as an antipasto or a side dish with fish.

Serves 6

5 tablespoons extra virgin olive oil
100g coarse dried breadcrumbs
1 red pepper, deseeded and cut into strips
1 yellow pepper, deseeded and cut into strips
1 green pepper, deseeded and cut into strips
2 cloves of garlic, finely chopped
a good handful of flat-leaf parsley, chopped
leaves from 2 sprigs of mint, chopped
2 tablespoons capers, rinsed if salted
salt and freshly ground black pepper
1 tablespoon white wine vinegar

Heat 2 tablespoons of olive oil over a medium heat. Add the breadcrumbs and stir continuously until they turn a handsome brown. Scrape out on to a plate and reserve.

Wipe out the pan, then return it to the heat with 3 tablespoons of olive oil. Heat through over a high heat, then add all the peppers and sauté until patched with brown and floppy. Add the garlic and cook for 1–2 minutes more. Turn off the heat. Stir in the herbs, capers, salt and pepper. Drizzle over the vinegar and mix. Now mix in just over half the breadcrumbs.

Taste and adjust the seasoning, adding more vinegar if you think it could do with pepping up.

Scrape into a serving dish and leave to cool. Just before serving, scatter over the rest of the crisp breadcrumbs.

Maria's Friggitelli al Pomodoro

Friggitelli Peppers with Tomato

Within a few days of moving into my little house in Ceglie Messapica, I met Maria, who lives below me on the ground floor. We discussed my rent (everyone here asks how much it is within minutes), the market, where to buy electric fans in anticipation of high summer heat, what I was doing here, the water-overflow from the air-conditioning which, if not checked, trickles down on her step.

Outside her front door, an enormous, vibrant pot of basil announces that this is the home of a serious cook. A day or so later proof arrived in the form of a small plastic bowl, wrapped in foil. In it a mess of fried green peppers, a seasoning of tomato, basil and garlic, glistening with olive oil. You cannot believe how delicious it was, better than anything I'd eaten in restaurants down the length of Italy.

Friggitelli al pomodoro is a dish that is commonplace throughout much of Italy, but Maria's version remains iconic. This is as near to it as I can get.

Unless you have access to genuine *friggitelli* peppers, replace them with Spanish-style Padrón peppers. Not the same, but the taste is something like. Serve as a side dish, hot or at room temperature, as part of an antipasto, or as a sauce for pasta. It will keep happily for 4 or 5 days, covered, in the fridge.

Serves 4

350g *friggitelli* or Padrón peppers
an enthusiastic 4 tablespoons of extra virgin olive oil
2 cloves of garlic, finely chopped
180g cherry or mini-plum tomatoes, halved or quartered if on the large side
a couple of pinches of dried chilli flakes (optional)
a big beautiful handful of basil leaves
salt and freshly ground black pepper

Trim the stalks off the peppers, but otherwise leave them whole. Heat the oil in a medium-sized frying pan until piping hot. Fry the peppers in the oil, turning frequently, until they are browned and softened. Now add the garlic, and stir for a few seconds until just beginning to brown. Throw in the tomatoes and the chilli flakes, if using, stir, then add the basil, salt and pepper. Turn down the heat, cover and cook for another 5–10 minutes.

Taste and add more salt and pepper as needed. Eat hot, warm or at room temperature.

A Lorry Load of Artichokes

Italy, I have read, is home to some 90 varieties of artichoke. Damn it, that's a lot. Thankfully most of them can be separated into just two categories: big and round or little and pointy. The big ones correspond to the globe artichokes that are, if not familiar, at least recognisable to people who don't live in continental Europe. The little ones, no bigger than the size of my fist, are by far and away the favourites down here in Puglia. From late autumn into spring they are everywhere, piled up vertiginously high, not only in shops but also on the little three-wheeled Ape vans that chunter around the narrow streets, so high on pickup trucks that they obscure the traffic lights, higher still on lorries. They travel complete with silvery green leaves and stem attached, most of which is stripped off by the vendors, generating enough compostable waste, you would have thought, to fertilise the whole of Puglia.

I am inevitably, regularly, seduced by their beauty and the prospect of a mouthful of their deliciousness. I forget for a few minutes that you get barely more than a mouthful from each one, and that's only when you have spent an age trimming off the tough bracts that hide the inner gem. Final outcome: another high mound of waste towering over a bowl of neat little artichoke hearts.

Anyway, all I really wanted to say here is that the two recipes that follow can be made with big or little artichokes and both are worth your time and an overflowing food waste caddy.

Preparing artichoke hearts, big or little

Begin by squeezing the juice of half a lemon into a bowl of cold water and then drop the squeezed lemon shell in there, too. Slice off the stems about 1cm below the body of the artichokes. Pop the main parts of the artichokes into the lemon water to slow down browning. Cut off the top 7–8cm of the stems and discard the rest. Peel with a vegetable peeler to remove all the tough fibrous outer layer. Slice at an angle to create long oval pieces 0.5cm thick. Scoop them into the acidulated water.

Now the artichokes themselves. Snap off the outer leaves, working your way around and around until you get to the softer inner leaves. Trim off the stubs. Turn the artichokes on their sides and cut off the cone, leaving about 2cm of leaf above the base. Quarter the artichokes and scrape out the hairy choke. In small Italian artichokes there won't be much, but globe artichokes will be more hirsute. Make sure you get rid of every last bit. Return the pieces to the lemony water.

There's no need to do any more to small Italian artichokes, but slice globe artichokes thickly. As soon as each piece is done, return it to the water bath.

Carciofi Fritti

Artichoke Fritters

You know you are in a good local restaurant when a plate of hot artichoke fritters turns up as part of an antipasto. Sometimes the little wedges of artichoke are swaddled in a doughy batter, but even better is this version, where they wear no more than a cloak of flour seasoned with Parmesan.

Serves 4–6 as part of an antipasto

100g plain flour
salt and freshly ground black pepper
30g freshly grated Parmesan
3–4 eggs
sunflower oil, for frying
6 small Italian artichokes or 2 globe artichokes, trimmed and prepared (see pages 34–35)
lemon wedges

Shortly before serving, mix together the flour, salt, pepper and Parmesan in a shallow bowl. Beat 3 eggs together lightly in another bowl (you may not need the last one, but good to have it to hand in case you run out). Arrange the flour and egg mixtures next to the hob. Line a large plate or a baking tray with three layers of kitchen paper. Pour 3cm or so of sunflower oil into a small pan and place over a moderate heat.

Drain the artichoke pieces and dry as well as you can in a clean tea towel. A few at a time, first toss them in the flour mixture, shaking off the excess, then coat thoroughly in egg, and finally return them to the flour to coat completely. Fry for about 5 minutes or so, until golden brown and tender. Scoop out and drain on the paper-lined plate. Serve swiftly while still crisp, with lemon wedges to squeeze over them.

Artichoke and Prawn Salad

There is something altogether excellent about the pairing of prawns and artichokes. This is a salad for warm spring days around the Mediterranean, or early summer in more northerly climes. Make sure that the dressing is vigorously lemony, and be generous with the mint leaves.

Serves 4 as a main course, 6 as a starter

6 small Italian artichokes or 2 globe artichokes, trimmed and prepared
150g new potatoes, halved
1 glass of dry white wine (around 120ml)
150ml chicken or vegetable stock, or water
6 flat-leaf parsley stems and a sprig of mint, tied together
2 cloves of garlic, sliced
salt and freshly ground black pepper
350g raw prawns, shelled and deveined if necessary
4 tablespoons extra virgin olive oil
1–2 lemons
2 good handfuls of salad leaves: cos lettuce, shredded, radicchio, shredded, frisée lettuce, torn into small pieces, or rocket, or a mixture of some or all of them
around 20 mint leaves, roughly chopped
2 tablespoons roughly chopped flat-leaf parsley

Put the prepared artichokes and new potatoes into a wide, deep skillet or frying pan in a single layer. Pour in the white wine and the stock. Tuck the bundle of parsley and mint in with them, add the garlic, and season with salt and pepper. Cover with a lid or foil and simmer over a gentle heat, stirring occasionally, until the artichokes and potatoes are just cooked – somewhere between 30 and 40 minutes. By this time there should be just a thin layer of liquid left in the pan. Scatter the prawns on top of the vegetables, clamp the lid back on and simmer for another 2–3 minutes, until just cooked through. Take the pan off the heat and let it cool for a few minutes. Throw out the bedraggled herbs. Spoon over 3 tablespoons of olive oil and squeeze in the juice of 1 lemon. Mix gently, then cool completely.

Shortly before serving, toss with the salad leaves, mint and parsley. Taste and adjust the seasonings, adding more lemon juice and olive oil as needed. Serve immediately while the flavours are at their best.

Le Cipolle al Forno di Olivia

Olivia's Roast Onions

Olivia and her husband, Roberto, run the small greengrocery right in the centre of Ceglie. She wears gold earrings, smiles a lot, and is generous with cooking tips and recipes. The first thing I bought from her was a skein of enormous red Tropea onions. This is how she likes to cook them. Serve as a side dish or part of an antipasto, or starter.

NB: I make double or treble the quantity of breadcrumbs, cheese and parsley. What I don't use immediately I freeze. They can be used (from frozen) on the next batch of onions, or on peppers (see page 30) or on a fillet of fish (raise the oven temperature to 220°C/200°C fan/gas 7).

Serves 4

1 Tropea onion or 2 well-proportioned round red onions
extra virgin olive oil
salt and freshly ground black pepper
25g stale, good-quality bread, torn into small chunks
a small handful of flat-leaf parsley
25g freshly grated Parmesan or pecorino

Preheat the oven to 200°C/180°C fan/gas 6.

Slice the onion into discs around 0.5cm thick. Smear the bottom of a baking dish enthusiastically with olive oil. Lay the onion rings on the oil, snuggling them close, overlapping slightly if necessary. Season with salt and lots of freshly ground black pepper.

Blitz the bread with the parsley to fine crumbs and mix in the cheese. Scatter the mixture thickly over the onions. Drizzle with a thread of olive oil, then bake for around 30 minutes, until sizzling hot and handsomely browned. Serve hot or at room temperature.

Wild asparagus, tame asparagus

I doubt that foraging would count as an essential reason to leave the house under coronavirus lockdown rules in the UK, but here in the south of Italy many see it as a 'situation of need' or indeed as a 'health reason'. In March, fields are rife with wild asparagus, and what right-thinking Italian would let that go to waste? No problem with social distancing out there, either.

Virtuously I haven't joined the throngs of foragers but I have been the beneficiary of their enthusiasm. I snaffled an orderly bunch of *asparagi selvatici* from the greengrocer at the bottom of the hill, then a few days later a plastic bag stuffed full of tangled twisting stems was thrust upon me by a friend. At arm's length of course.

The two look distinctly different. Orderly bunch must have been picked when they were young and ramrod straight, with a close resemblance to cultivated asparagus, just thinner and darker in colour. The taste is decidedly asparagussy with a fetching hint of bitterness to them, a tad less sweet and juicy. Disorderly, tangled ragbag, on the other hand, is mostly vivid green, has barely a straight stem to its name, and sports any number of thready side shoots. This stuff is a few days more mature than orderly bunch, has experienced a longer wilder life and in my opinion is all the better for it (kind of like human beings; I've always preferred the less orderly ones). Sure, it takes more work to extract the tender tip, there's more woody stem in the bin, but the flavour is bigger, more asparagussy still and has just the perfect, clear bitter edge to it.

As usual, local opinion varies on how best to use it. Almost everyone votes keenly for a frittata, but the thorny issue of cheese (none/*cacioricotta*/Parmesan/pecorino) divides them again. Wild asparagus with pasta? NO, NO, YES, YES. Just blanched and served with olive oil and a spritz of lemon?

Yeeees, but not so sure about the lemon. Roasted or grilled with olive oil and Parmesan? Foreigners are just weird (full agreement on this one). I don't even bother querying stir-frying or dousing in melted butter.

So far, so expected, but the big discovery, the one that knocks me for six, is the epic frittata made by Loredana. Loredana is small, dynamic, bouncy, hoots with laughter, and makes her own sourdough bread. She also makes a frittata with the most delicious, crunchy crust to it. I am in love with the bread and frittata, and her, at first bite. I have never tasted a frittata like this before.

The key, she explains, is bread. Just like when you make *polpette di pane* (see page 167). You soften it in water, squeeze it dry, then beat it into the egg and cheese mixture (yes, she's all for the cheese) before adding a mountain of lightly cooked wild asparagus. It sounds so simple, but it takes me endless attempts to get it anywhere near as good as hers.

How to prepare wild asparagus and what to use when you can't get it

The first thing to do with your wild asparagus, or indeed any asparagus, is to give it a good rinse under the cold tap, paying particular attention to the tips. Shake off what moisture you can and leave it to dry if you are going to fry or grill it.

Wild asparagus has a bigger proportion of tough woody stem than cultivated. Since it is thinner, it is pretty easy to feel your way down to the point where it is beginning to toughen. Snap the hard stuff off and discard. If it is beginning to sprout spindly side shoots, check these out. Some will be fine to add to the pot, but others will be wiry and should be rejected.

When you can't lay your hands on wild asparagus, i.e. most of the time, you can replace it with 'sprue', the thinnest, early cultivated asparagus that used to be sold off cheap, but now gets a cute-factor price hike. It doesn't have the wild bitterness, but it tastes good anyway. It may need a minute more cooking time.

Frittata di Asparagi Selvatici

Wild/Sprue Asparagus Frittata (cooked in a frying pan)

You might imagine that adding bread to a frittata would make it heavy and dull, but if anything, it is the opposite. Think of it more as omelette meets eggy bread, with its lovely tender centre. You need to start off with a good-quality bread, of course, but the stale end of a loaf is absolutely fine.

Cooking the asparagus first in oil and then adding a splash of water to soften it means that you preserve every last mite of its flavour, instead of abandoning it in a pan of bubbling water. It works just as well with sprue as with wild asparagus. For thicker asparagus, add a little more water, and stir around once or twice as it softens.

Be brave with the heat and the oil.

Serves 2 as a main course, 4–6 as part of an antipasto

110–120g thick slices of stale, good-quality bread
3 tablespoons extra virgin olive oil
100–130g trimmed wild asparagus or fine sprue asparagus, cut into 5cm lengths
salt and freshly ground black pepper
4 eggs
15g freshly grated Parmesan
2 tablespoons finely chopped flat-leaf parsley

Trim the crusts off the bread. You will need 60g crustless weight. Tear up roughly, and soak in cold water for 4 or 5 minutes. Drain and squeeze out most of the water.

Heat a tablespoon of olive oil in a small frying pan (24cm diameter) over a low to moderate heat. Add the asparagus and fry gently for a minute or two, turning the stems so that they are all coated in oil. Now add 3 tablespoons of water and a little salt. Cover and leave to simmer for 4–5 minutes. Remove the lid. If there is still some water left in the pan, cook for a few minutes more to drive it off. Now tip the asparagus into a bowl and set aside. Don't wash the frying pan yet.

While the asparagus is cooking, beat the soaked bread with the eggs, Parmesan, parsley, salt and lots of freshly ground black pepper. Break the lumps up as you mix to produce a thick and fairly homogeneous mixture. Stir in the cooked asparagus as soon as it's tepid. Return the frying pan to a lively heat, add another tablespoon of olive oil, and get it spanking hot. Pour in the egg mixture. Stir the mixture briefly, then cook for a few minutes. Reduce the heat a little, cover with a lid and leave to cook for 3–4 minutes until the underneath is browned, and the top is almost but not quite set.

Loosen the edges with your spatula if necessary, then cover the frying pan with a lid and with a quick flick of the wrist invert the two together so that the frittata drops on to the lid. Return the frying pan to the heat, add the last tablespoon of oil and, once it is hot, slide the frittata back into it. Cook until the underneath is golden brown. Slide out on to a plate and eat warm or at room temperature.

Frittata d'Agretti, al Forno

Oven-cooked Agretti Frittata

At last I found the key to making a crisp-topped frittata like Loredana's. It's simple and obvious once you know. You just bake it in the oven, topped with an extra layer of dried breadcrumbs and plenty of extra virgin olive oil.

In this version I've included *agretti* (monk's beard), which is fine enough to need no pre-cooking, but it's easily adapted to other vegetables – try it with grated courgettes, salted first to get rid of most of their water, or with just-wilted spinach, squeezed hard to eliminate unwanted liquid.

Serves 4–6

80g stale, good-quality bread
80–100g *agretti*
6 eggs
30g freshly grated Parmesan, pecorino or *cacioricotta*
2 tablespoons finely chopped flat-leaf parsley
salt and freshly ground black pepper
4 tablespoons extra virgin olive oil
25g dried breadcrumbs

Preheat the oven to 180°C/160°C fan/gas 4.

Soak the bread in cold water for 5 minutes. Meanwhile, rinse the *agretti* and pat off excess water with a few pieces of kitchen paper. Discard the thickest stems and chop the rest very roughly.

Back to the bread: drain and squeeze out most of the water. Place the squeezed bread in a mixing bowl and break the eggs in on top. Add the Parmesan, parsley, salt and pepper and 1 tablespoon of olive oil. Beat the whole lot together, breaking up the chunks of bread, until you have a pappy mixture. It doesn't have to be smooth, but there should no longer be any evidence of large globs of bread. Stir in the *agretti*.

Find a heavy-based, ovenproof frying pan, 23cm across, or a small roasting tin roughly 20cm square. Pour in 1 tablespoon of olive oil and smear it around the base and sides. Scrape in the frittata mixture and smooth down. Now sprinkle over the breadcrumbs as evenly as you can, making sure they go right up to the edge. Drizzle the remaining 2 tablespoons of olive oil over the top. Whip the pan into the oven and bake for 20 minutes, until the top is crisp and the egg is cooked through.

Eat warm or at room temperature, cut into wedges or squares.

Frittata di Prezzemolo e Menta

Parsley and Mint Frittata

This is the simplest form of frittata, made in a matter of minutes, with oodles of fresh herbs, eggs, cheese. *Basta così!* Enough!

Serves 4–6 as part of an antipasto

4 eggs
15g freshly grated pecorino, Parmesan or *cacioricotta*
3 heaped tablespoons finely chopped flat-leaf parsley
2 heaped tablespoons chopped mint
1 clove of garlic, crushed
salt and freshly ground black pepper
3 tablespoons extra virgin olive oil

Whisk the eggs with the pecorino, parsley, mint, garlic, salt and lots of freshly ground black pepper.

Heat 2 tablespoons of olive oil in a 22–23cm frying pan until very hot. Pour in the egg mixture. Stir briefly, then reduce the heat a little and leave to cook for 3–4 minutes, until the underneath is browned and the top is almost but not quite set.

Loosen the edges with your spatula if necessary, then cover the frying pan with a lid and, with a quick flick of the wrist, invert the two together so that the frittata drops on to the lid. Return the frying pan to the heat and add the last tablespoon of oil. As soon as it is good and hot, slide the frittata back into it. Cook until the underneath is golden brown. Slide out on to a plate and eat warm or at room temperature.

Fave e Cicoria

Bean Purée with Bitter Greens

One of the classic Puglian dishes on every restaurant menu, and probably on every old-fashioned home menu, is *fave e cicoria*. A rich broad bean purée (made from dried broad beans), served with boiled greens, usually but not exclusively, *cicoria*. Spinach makes a fine, if inauthentic, substitute. It doesn't sound like much, but when it is good, on a chilly spring night, it is phenomenal. Comfort food, *cucina povera*, not too pretty, but satisfying to soul and taste-buds simultaneously.

In the UK, you may be able to get dried fava beans from Italian delis, but they're also often sold in Greek groceries. Try to find the split, skinned beans. You may have to settle for whole beans, in which case they will have to be skinned after soaking. Tedious, but essential.

Serves 4

250g dried, skinned broad beans (*fave*)
2 cloves of garlic, smashed and skinned
1 large or 2 medium-sized potatoes, peeled and sliced
extra virgin olive oil
salt and freshly ground black pepper

For the cicoria
300–500g *cicoria*, trimmed, or 500g spinach
2 cloves of garlic, finely chopped
extra virgin olive oil

Soak the beans in cold water for a good 12 hours. Drain and tip into a saucepan. Add the garlic and lay the potato slices on top (they'll keep the beans under the water). Pour in enough cold water to cover by a finger knuckle's depth. Bring up to the boil and simmer for 30–40 minutes, until the beans and potatoes are soft enough to crush against the side of the pan. Check regularly and add a little more water if it threatens to dry out.

If you are feeling energetic, beat the beans and potatoes with a wooden spoon to produce a rough purée. Alternatively, take the easy route and purée with an immersion blender in the pan. Add a great big slurp of olive oil, and a decent wallop of salt. Stir over a moderate heat until the purée is thick enough to stand a spoon up in it. Reheat when needed.

For the *cicoria*, rinse it well to remove any trapped grit. Trim off the tough ends and cut into 10–15cm lengths. Simmer in salted boiling water until very tender – 10–15 minutes. Drain. Just before serving, fry the chopped garlic in plenty of olive oil until just turning brown at the edges, add the *cicoria*, and toss in the garlicky oil until hot, hot, hot.

If using spinach, cook it lightly and leave to drain in a sieve, then reheat as if it were *cicoria*.

Serve a big helping each of steaming hot fava bean purée, with a heap of *cicoria* or spinach perched on top. Finish with a drizzle of best olive oil.

Il Finocchio al Forno di Mia Mamma

My Mother's Baked Fennel

In the early 1950s my mother travelled for several months around Italy. How extraordinary that must have seemed to a young woman fresh from university, with memories of the war still vivid and raw. I wish now that I had talked to her more about her experience. I assume that she went for the art, but I know that the food made a lasting impact on her. How could it not, after a decade of food rationing? Among the many Italian dishes she cooked for our family as I was growing up, two stand out above the rest: grilled pepper salads and baked fennel, drenched with butter and Parmesan. You don't really need a proper recipe for this; just be enthusiastic with the butter and cheese.

fennel bulbs
salt and freshly ground black pepper
butter
freshly grated Parmesan

Preheat the oven to 200°C/180°C fan/gas 6.

Trim the fennel, slicing off the fibrous stem ends. Cut into wedges – 4 if the bulbs are relatively small, 8 or more if large. Cook in a pan of salted boiling water until tender. Drain really, really, really thoroughly, pressing down gently on the tender fennel with your hands to get rid of water trapped in the layers.

Butter an ovenproof dish generously. Lay the fennel in the dish, no more than a couple of layers thick. Season with freshly ground black pepper. Dot generously with butter, then dredge with a blanket of Parmesan. Bake for 20–25 minutes, until the cheese has browned and the butter is sizzling cheerfully.

Let it cool for a few minutes, then serve with wedges of bread to mop up the buttery juices.

2

(ALMOST) THE NOISIEST PLACE IN TOWN

Macelleria da Franco is just a few yards down the street from my house. It's a small, well-kept butcher's shop with a constant stream of customers popping in and out. Franco himself comes straight out of the classic butchers' mould, albeit with Italian seasoning. He's stocky and strong, a round genial face, not much hair. It's not the smartest butchery in town, but the meat is good quality and mostly local, there's a fine display of dark, long-hung ribs of beef in a temperature-controlled unit and the prices are reasonable.

For me it's a place of discovery and of sleeplessness during the hot summer months. While I wait for Franco to mince the meat for the *polpette* (see page 59) I'm about to make, I pass the time chatting to formidable local cooks about the way they make them. With garlic or without? Pecorino or Parmesan? Parsley, onion, ratio of breadcrumbs to meat, egg or no egg? They all have their strong opinions on the matter and are delighted to educate an ignorant foreigner on the best way forward. Not mentioned, because to them it is just how it is always done, is the fact that the meat must be freshly minced to order. Were Franco to offer them a prepacked tray of mince, greying slightly at the edges, they would turn sharply on their heels and exit in horror. Of course, he never would. I doubt it even occurs to him that this might be a time-saver.

Like so many butchers' shops round here, his small kingdom takes on a whole new groove as the long, hot summer nights set in. In partnership with the pocket-handkerchief-sized Bar del Teatro next door, it spills out on to the street. Half a dozen or so trestle tables are set up and customers clamour for paninis filled with his freshly cooked sausages or *bombette* or whatever else emerges from the ovens, washed down with an icy beer. And they just keep on clamouring as they squeeze on to the benches.

Entire families cluster round the tables, *nonna* and *nonno*, parents, cousins, aunts and uncles, young children, babies and toddlers, laughing, shouting and singing as they make the most of the relative cool of the night. *'Anto, Anto, vieni qua!'* calls a mother to a child lost entirely in his game of hide and seek with a friend. *Vieni qua*, come here. It's a phrase you hear like an infinite echo throughout Italy, in the small squares and back-streets, mothers calling in their children to eat, to take siesta, to run an errand for them.

At one thirty in the morning it echoes up to me in my bedroom, a phrase I understand through the loud babble, mostly in dialect, from the street outside Franco's *macelleria*. A minute later it's followed by a wail from the child as he's dragged away from the fun. It's the beginning of the end of the party, and a signal that I may, eventually, be able to sleep, and that Franco will finally be closing shop.

Polpette di Carne

Meatballs

Polpette di carne pop up again and again on Puglian tables, on their own, plain and unadorned to nibble with drinks, as part of an antipasto, or with pasta, as in the Mandurian *orecchiette al Primitivo* recipe on page 173, in tomato *sugo*, or in Maria's fabulous *pasta al forno* (see page 170).

Makes loads

300g minced beef, veal or pork
75g freshly grated pecorino or Parmesan
75g soft or slightly stale breadcrumbs (crusts included)
2–3 tablespoons finely chopped flat-leaf parsley
2 cloves of garlic, crushed
1 egg, lightly beaten
lots of freshly ground black pepper (and salt if needed)
extra virgin olive oil, for frying

Mix the minced beef, cheese, breadcrumbs, parsley, garlic, egg and pepper thoroughly with your hands. Really work and knead it well, to make a cohesive, rollable mix. Don't add salt yet – the cheese will probably have already done the job. Check this by rolling a small knob of the mixture into a mini-patty and frying it in a miserly smear of oil. Taste and adjust the seasoning accordingly. Now that's sorted, roll the rest of the mixture into small balls (see notes on page 60).

Heat 2 tablespoons of olive oil in a wide frying pan over a moderately lively heat. Add the *polpette* (you should hear a hissing sizzle as they hit the oil – if you don't, then it isn't hot enough). Fry for a few minutes without disturbing, then shake the pan gently, to roll them over. Fry until browned, then scoop out on to a plate lined with kitchen paper. Eat while still warm or set aside.

Notes

For nibbles with drinks, or as part of an antipasto, roll into small balls, roughly 1.5cm across.

To add to *orecchiette al Primitivo* (see page 173), or for *pasta al sugo con polpette di carne,* roll them a little bigger, say 2–2.5cm.

To add to composite baked pasta dishes (such as Maria's Ferragosta *pasta al forno,* see page 170), roll small, 1.5cm again.

Bombette

Little Pork, Pancetta and Cheese Parcels

Bombette, little bombs, are rolls of very thin meat, pork or beef or veal, bundled up with ham, cheese or herbs or all three. They are an essential part of the Puglian meat fest. When Puglians eat out or gather together for special family occasions, there is nothing better than an outrageous quantity of meats, preferably cooked over a beltingly-hot wood fire. As well as the little bombs clustered on skewers, there will be *fegatini,* little liver faggots rolled in caul fat, also spiked on skewers, beef steak, lamb chops, sausages, and just occasionally a little bit of chicken, but all in absurd abundance. Italian friends think me a total wimp when I insist that I couldn't possibly force down another scrap of charred flesh, so I politely resort to another *bombetta* to keep them happy.

At home, I find that 4 *bombette* per person is quite adequate. If *caciocavallo* is not available, use any decent melty cheese. I like to eat the oozing little bombs on a mound of mashed potato, with plenty of green veg on the side. It's not at all how it is done here, but I like something more than just meat and a waft of green salad as an accompaniment. They're also good on *pasta pomodoro,* pasta with tomato sauce.

Serves 4 non-Pugliese

8 thin slices of pork shoulder (weighing around 475–550g altogether)
freshly ground black pepper
8 thin slices of pancetta, cut in half
16 whole flat-leaf parsley leaves
80–100g *caciocavallo* or *provolone picante,* or Gruyère or even Cheddar, cut into slim batons, roughly 4cm long

a little extra virgin olive oil
wedges of lemon, for serving

One at a time, sandwich each slice of pork between 2 sheets of baking parchment. Use a rolling pin or the smooth side of a meat mallet to thwack them out until they are at least doubled in size and verging on paper-thin.

Cut each one in half and lay them out side by side on your chopping board. Season with freshly ground black pepper, but no need for salt. Lay a half slice of pancetta on each one and pop a parsley leaf on top of that towards the end nearest you. Lay a baton of cheese across that. Now fold in the sides of the pork slices over the ends of the cheese batons, then roll them up as neatly as you can. Spear them on skewers to keep them from unravelling.

Either grill them on the barbecue, brushed with a little oil, not too close to the heat so that they have time to cook right through. Or roast in a preheated oven, 200°C/180°C fan/gas 6, brushed lightly with oil, for 20 minutes or so. Or remove carefully from the skewers and fry slowly in olive oil over a lowish heat until browned.

Serve with wedges of lemon to squeeze over them.

Polpettone Ripieno

Mozzarella-stuffed Meatloaf

Here's another cook's thing I've learnt the hard way. Minced beef in Italy is much leaner than minced beef in the UK, and that means it needs a bit more tlc in the kitchen. My first attempt at a *polpettone* was not a disaster but it wasn't too great either. Flavour fine, texture dry. Friends were polite and avowed that they liked it, but I knew it was poor stuff compared to the *polpettone* I had eaten a few months earlier downstairs in Maria's house.

This is the massively improved revamped version, moistened with milk-soaked bread and finely chopped mortadella. It's suitable for leaner beef, but frankly it's even better made with 5–10% fat minced beef. Fat, as always, is the key to flavour and texture when it comes to meat.

Meatloaf is as much a standard of family meals here in the deep south of Italy as it is in the USA, and comes complete with a thousand and one variations. Locally, it seems that mortadella is the preferred way of adding richness to the meat (surprisingly and somewhat dismayingly, it contains roughly as much fat as pancetta, which is an acceptable alternative). Billeted somewhere in the centre is a thick, oozy band of mozzarella or *scamorza* cheese, capers for piquancy, and parsley. Nice.

Serves 6–8

olive oil, for greasing the dish
80g stale bread
6 tablespoons milk
100g mortadella (or pancetta)
130g mozzarella, smoked mozzarella or *scamorza*

800g minced beef or half-and-half minced beef and veal
80g freshly grated pecorino or Parmesan
3 tablespoons finely chopped flat-leaf parsley
3 cloves of garlic, crushed
2 eggs
salt and lots of freshly ground black pepper
a small handful of whole flat-leaf parsley leaves
1 tablespoon capers, rinsed if salted

And also
3–4 medium-sized potatoes, cut into wedges
extra virgin olive oil

Preheat the oven to 180°C/160°C fan/gas 4. Grease a moderately large baking dish with a little oil.

Tear the bread into chunks (crust and all, unless it is impossibly thick and tough) and soak in the milk until softened. Mash the two together roughly. Set aside 3 slices of mortadella and chop the rest finely. Cut the mozzarella into 1cm-thick slices, then cut again to form 1cm-thick batons.

Add the soggy bread and milk and chopped mortadella to the minced beef along with the pecorino or Parmesan, chopped parsley, garlic, eggs, salt and pepper. Mix the whole lot together.

Tear off a large rectangle of baking parchment and lay it flat on the work surface. Tip the meat out in a heap in the middle. Pat it out firmly to form a large rectangle some 1.5cm thick. Arrange the mozzarella batons in a long line parallel to and about 3cm away from one of the narrower sides of your rectangle. Arrange the whole parsley leaves on top of the mozzarella, then scatter over the capers.

Now roll up the meatloaf, lifting the meat up and over the mozzarella with the help of the baking parchment. Lift the rolled meatloaf, still in its paper jacket, into the oiled baking dish, and roll it into place as you remove the baking parchment. Toss the potato wedges with 2 tablespoons of olive oil and season with salt. Arrange them around the meatloaf. Brush the meatloaf with a little olive oil, then slide into the oven.

Roast for 50–70 minutes (the thicker it is the longer it will take), turning the potatoes a couple of times and basting the meatloaf with its own juices. Check that the meatloaf is done by inserting a skewer into the centre: if the juices run pink, cook for another 10 minutes or so. If they are clear, it is done. If you use a meat thermometer, it should register 70°C.

Take the meatloaf out of the oven, cover loosely with foil and leave to rest for 10 minutes before slicing and serving with the potato wedges.

Pignata di Manzo

Beef (or Pork) and Red Wine Stew

This is an excellent tomatoey stew, braised slowly to soften the fibres and bring out the flavour of the meat. The classic Puglian version is made with horse meat cooked overnight in an earthenware pot, the *pignata*, in the dying embers of the bread oven. Although I've eaten it in restaurants I just can't bring myself to buy *puledro*, foal, to cook at home. Hypocritical, I know, but we all have our boundaries.

So beef it is, or occasionally pork, with lots and lots of deep red sauce which is often served first on pasta, with the meat dished up afterwards.

Serves 6

4 tablespoons extra virgin olive oil
1 onion, sliced
1 carrot, finely diced
1 stem of celery, thinly sliced
4 cloves of garlic, sliced
3 red chillies, fresh or dried, chopped
1kg chuck or rump beef or pork, cut into 5cm chunks
150ml red or white wine
800g passata
2 bay leaves
10 sage leaves
a small bunch of flat-leaf parsley, chopped, stalks and all
salt and freshly ground black pepper
600g potatoes

Preheat the oven to 150°C/130°C fan/gas 2.

Put the olive oil into a flameproof and ovenproof casserole dish with the onion, carrot, celery, garlic and chillies. Cook over a moderate heat until the vegetables are tender, then raise the heat and add the meat. Brown it as well as you can, without letting your *soffritto* of vegetables burn. Pour in the wine and let it sizzle up and boil for a minute or so.

Pour in the passata and 400ml of water, add the herbs and season with salt and pepper. Bring to the boil, then cover with a lid and transfer to the oven. Leave it to cook for around 2 hours, until the meat is tender. Check occasionally and give it a good stir.

Meanwhile, peel the potatoes and cut into large chunks. Add to the casserole, together with a splash or two of water if the sauce has thickened too much – a *pignata* has far more sauce than a standard beef stew, so it will probably need it. Cover and return to the oven for 45 minutes or so, until the potatoes are cooked through.

Serve most of the sauce on pasta, with the meat and potatoes to follow.

Agnello ai Piselli e Limone

Lemony Lamb Stew with Peas

This begins as a fairly standard lamb stew, with a bevy of vegetables, pancetta and wine, but what transforms it into an outstanding delight is the final touch. Egg yolks and lemon juice are whisked into the fully cooked stew, thickening it lightly and bringing a silky sharpness with it. You'll find the same thing across the Adriatic in Greece (*avgolemono*), but this is the Italian way.

Serves 6

1.5kg leg of lamb, boned-out weight, cut into large chunks
3 tablespoons extra virgin olive oil
1 onion, sliced
80g pancetta, cut into cubes
3 tablespoons chopped flat-leaf parsley
150ml dry white wine
salt and freshly ground black pepper
400g peas (frozen work very nicely if you can't get/haven't the patience for fresh)
4 egg yolks
juice of 1½ lemons

Preheat the oven to 150°C/130°C fan/gas 2.

Trim the meat as needed. Put half the olive oil in a frying pan together with the onion and pancetta and fry over a medium heat until the onion is tender and floppy. Meanwhile heat the remaining oil in a casserole dish and brown the lamb roughly in it in several batches. When the pancetta and onion are cooked, add them to the casserole, along with most of the parsley, too. Save a little parsley for a final garnish.

Deglaze the frying pan with the white wine – in other words, return the frying pan to the heat, pour in the white wine and bring to the boil, scraping in all the residue caught on the base of the pan. Pour this over the lamb and season with salt and pepper. Cover, transfer to the oven and cook for some 1–2 hours, or until the meat is very tender. Stir in the peas and cook for another 3 or 4 minutes.

Whisk the egg yolks with the lemon juice. Take the lamb stew out of the oven and pour in the egg and lemon mixture. Stir until it thickens to form a smooth sauce. Scatter over the remaining parsley and serve immediately.

A Curious Absence of Chickens

One of the reasons I chose to settle in Ceglie Messapica is that it has no great claims to fame. Its *centro storico* is charmingly full of twists and turns and white-painted ancient houses but can't hold a candle to Ostuni's stunning medieval maze of a centre some eight miles closer to the coast. The small *palazzo ducale* has been clad in scaffolding since the day I arrived, but even without it I can't imagine that it would be much of a tourist magnet. The churches are handsome but not remarkable. In short, it is a proper working town inhabited by proper working families.

What Ceglie does have, however, is an exceptionally large number of restaurants for a town with a mere 20,000 inhabitants. How many? It's hard to tell but I reckon that there must be around forty to fifty if you include the edge-of-town party places. Among this crowd are one Michelin-starred restaurant and one Michelin-bibbed restaurant. The point is that Ceglie merits its self-appointed title of La Città della Gastronomia.

If you were to draw a Venn diagram of the types of restaurant it would be very simple. One large circle (Puglian cooking) and one medium-sized circle (*pizzerias*), with a minor but significant overlap, and next to them one tiny circle (the burger restaurant in Largo Ognissanto and the *kebabberia*).

I reckon that I've eaten my way through almost half of the Ceglie restaurant line-up now, as well as a fair number in other parts of Puglia. I have never once seen a chicken dish on any menu. Not once. How strange is that? Near the coast there's always plenty of fish on offer, but just a few miles inland it's meat, meat, meat all the way, by which I mean red meat: beef, lamb, horse or donkey. Pork makes its mark in the form of sausages, cured hams, salamis and the like.

It's not that you can't buy chicken in the butchers' shops or the supermarket. They sell some chicken but it is obviously not a majorly popular choice. My butcher, Franco, occasionally has one enticing yellow-fleshed chicken, complete with head and feet, on display in his shop, but it looks lonely and unloved.

Coming from the UK, where chicken is consumed in enormous quantity, I find this perplexing. One local friend suggests that it is because chicken was once the food of the poor, a slightly shameful taste, and not suitable for celebratory meals out in a restaurant. This seems plausible until I recall eating *orecchiette alle cime di rapa* (see page 165), *cavatelli* with black chickpeas, *fave e cicoria* (see page 51) and *marretti* (bundles of offal wrapped in caul fat) in hot, tightly packed trattorias. These are all indisputably dishes that emerge from poverty. Quite rightly the Pugliese are proud of them. So much for theory number one.

The Pugliese comedian and film actor, Checco Zalone, gave me a lead. His humour is warm and affectionate, highlighting the quirks and characteristics of Italian family life, poking fun at the north/south stereotypes. His 2016 comedy *Quo Vado* is a gentle gem, following the fortunes and misfortunes of a self-satisfied, chauvinist southern Italian civil servant who gradually becomes more 'woke' as he is sent to ever more distant posts. It is also Italy's highest grossing film ever, at least pre-Covid.

His song 'Lu Pollu Cusutu N'Culu' is a chicken's angry lament (in dialect) as it is being stuffed.

'Nu peperuncinu da sulu
Ci pizzica in bucca a nu mulu
Tu pensa a lu poveru pollu
Che se lu pijja intr'allu culu.'

'Just one lone hot chilli
Is enough to burn a donkey's mouth
Think then of this poor chicken
That's having it shoved up his arse.'

Here it was – the first example of a traditional Puglian chicken recipe, enshrined in verse. Hallelujah!

Stitched-up Arse Chicken is a strictly home affair. It's a domestic dish for family get-togethers to celebrate special occasions. Before the 1950s any poor household lucky enough to own a few chickens cherished them. A regular supply of free eggs was a regular supply of protein in a world where most couldn't afford meat or cheese. Only a remarkable event, like the *festa* of the local patron saint, warranted the sacrifice of even an old hen. Once a year it was worth it.

This, I believe, is the real reason why chicken never appears on restaurant menus nor in Puglian cookbooks. A laying chicken was just too precious to kill off. Old worn-out hens were too tough to roast or fry, so were good only for broth and lengthy simmering to render the sinewy meat edible. Italians cleave fiercely to traditions, especially here in the south. It will be a long time until chicken supremes make their way on to the official Puglian menu.

Lu Pollu Cusutu N'Culu

Stitched-up Arse Chicken

There are many, many different versions of this dish, depending on what was available to each cook, and what they could afford. If you had a little cash to spare, there would be meat and lots of cheese in the stuffing, but when times were truly hard, a few herbs, a handful of chillies and an onion might be all that lodged inside the chicken. Adding stale bread soaked in water to the stuffing mixture made the meal stretch further, filling the bellies of families more used to sparsity.

In other words, you should feel free to adapt the stuffing to your liking. Prefer pancetta to mortadella? Parmesan to pecorino? Go for it. Rosemary, thyme or dried oregano are good additions. Make it your own.

Serves 6–8

extra virgin olive oil
1 large free-range chicken (1.25–1.5kg)
1 large glass of white wine
salt and freshly ground black pepper

For the stuffing
2 chicken livers, roughly chopped
75ml dry white wine
60g mortadella, chopped
60g chunks of stale, good-quality bread
200g minced beef, veal or pork
2–3 tablespoons finely chopped flat-leaf parsley
2 cloves of garlic, finely chopped
4 fresh or dried red chillies, deseeded and finely chopped

45g freshly grated pecorino
1 egg

For the sauce
1 onion, sliced
400g cherry tomatoes, halved, or plum tomatoes, roughly chopped, or 1 x 400g tin of chopped tomatoes
a pinch or two of sugar if needed

You will also need a fairly sturdy needle and some white thread (or a couple of wooden cocktail sticks).

Preheat the oven to 200°C/180°C fan/gas 6.

To make the stuffing, heat a slug of olive oil in a frying pan. Add the chicken livers and fry for 4–5 minutes, until browned. Pour in the wine and cook for a minute or two more until it has virtually all evaporated. Stir in the mortadella. Take off the heat, scrape into a cool bowl and mash roughly with a fork. Leave to cool.

Cover the bread with water and set aside for a minute or two to soften. Put the minced beef into a bowl. Squeeze the water out of the bread and add to the beef, along with the chicken liver mixture, the parsley, garlic, chillies, pecorino and egg. Season generously with salt and pepper and mix the whole lot together. Fry a small knob of the mixture in a little oil. Taste and see if it needs more seasoning. Adjust accordingly.

Fill the central cavity of the chicken with this mixture, packing it in firmly. Now thread up that needle and tie the two ends of thread together in a knot. Sew up the opening of the chicken, so that none of the stuffing can fall out. Or just take the easy route and use a couple of cocktail sticks to tack the edges of the skin together.

Oil a roasting tin and tumble in all the sauce ingredients (if using). Sit the chicken in the tin. Drizzle over a little more oil, rubbing it in all over the skin. Pour over the wine, then season with salt and pepper. Roast for around 1½ hours, basting the chicken occasionally with its own juices. Add a splash or two of water if the tin threatens to dry out.

Check the chicken to make sure that it is cooked right through either by pushing a food thermometer, if you have one, into the heart of the stuffing (once it registers 75°C, it's ready) or by pushing a metal skewer into the centre of the stuffing. Leave for 30 seconds then pull out. Lay the tip on the inside of your wrist. If it's hot then you're good to go. Double-check by pushing the skewer into the thickest part of the chicken, down on the thigh. If the juices run clear, then the flesh is cooked through. If they're pink, pop the chicken back into the oven for another 10 minutes or so and repeat.

Once the chicken is cooked, cover loosely with foil and let it sit in a warm place for 10 minutes. Remove the thread or cocktail sticks, then divide the chicken up into chunky pieces. Serve together with big scoops of stuffing, and the delicious tomatoey goo.

Chickens and Football

A lively red and black *gallo* (rooster) is the symbol of Bari's much-loved football team. In April 2018, they were scheduled to play a match with arch-rivals Pescara. Bari's coach, who happened to live nearer Pescara than Bari, woke up the morning before the match to find his house daubed with graffiti and a dead cockerel swinging from a rope. The match was a diplomatic 2–2 draw. No mention of what happened to the corpse of the rooster but with any luck some enterprising cook popped it into a kitchen pot before the police claimed it as evidence.

My Spatchcocked Chicken with Lemon, Garlic and Black Olives

Spatchcocking and roasting is probably my all-time favourite method of cooking chicken, and I've been doing it this way for decades. Those Italian friends who are anxious about anything out of the ordinary food-wise feel comfortable when confronted with a dish of crisp-skinned chicken, suffused with lemon, garlic and olives. Practically Puglian, even if it is cooked for them by an English woman.

Be sure to get good-quality black olives for this. Cheap ready-stoned olives often taste soapy, so steer clear unless it's a brand you already know and enjoy. Better to start with whole olives, ones that you really like the taste of, and take the time to stone them yourself. The easiest way to do this is to press down firmly on each olive with the back of a wooden spoon to split it open. The stone then lifts out easily. You won't need all the olive mixture for your chicken, so scoop out about a third and store it in the fridge. It goes well with fish, or thin it down with a little more oil and serve with crisp fingers of carrot, celery, red pepper or fennel to dip into it, like French tapenade.

Serves 4 generously

1 lemon
170g black olives, stoned
2 cloves of garlic, roughly chopped
3 tablespoons roughly chopped flat-leaf parsley
85–110ml extra virgin olive oil, plus a little extra
1 medium free-range chicken

coarse salt and freshly ground black pepper
3 medium-sized potatoes, cut into wedges
2 red peppers, deseeded and cut into strips
or:
2 heads of fennel, trimmed and quartered
or:
4 carrots, cut in half lengthways

Preheat the oven to 190°C/170°C fan/gas 5.

Grate the zest of the lemon finely. Put it into a food processor with the olives, garlic and parsley. Process until finely chopped, then gradually trickle in the olive oil, with the blades of the motor still running, until you have a thick cream. Scrape down the sides and base and give the whole lot one last blast. Set aside about a third of the mixture in the fridge to use over the next few days.

Now for the chicken: turn the bird breast side down, then, using poultry shears or a sharp, strong knife, cut along the backbone from neck to tail end. Turn the chicken skin side up, then flatten it out firmly with the heel of your hand to form a butterfly shape (well, vaguely, anyway). Oil a roasting tin large enough to take the flattened chicken, with room to spare.

Now the messy bit. With your fingers, separate the skin from the flesh of the bird at the neck end. Wiggle your fingers about inside, pulling away the skin, but leaving it tethered at the sides, to form a pocket over the chicken. Spoon and smear around the black olive mixture between the flesh and skin, patting it down so that it spreads all over. Don't worry that it looks a bit mucky. It will all turn out well in the end. Squeeze over the juice of half the lemon, and season the skin with salt and pepper, rubbing it in. Finally drizzle over another tablespoon of olive oil.

Tuck the potato wedges and other vegetables around the chicken, season with salt and pepper, squeeze over the remaining lemon juice, and add a touch more oil. Turn the potatoes so that they are coated.

Roast for 45–60 minutes, until the chicken is cooked through, basting once or twice with its own juices. If it looks at all dry, add a splash or two of water. Check that the bird is done by plunging a skewer into the thickest part, between thigh and breast. If the juices run clear then the bird is ready, but if they run pink, it needs more time in the oven.

Using a sharp knife, hack the roasty toasty bird into quarters. Serve with the vegetables and give everyone permission to use their hands to tear the tender, salty chicken flesh apart.

3

FIVE HUNDRED MILES OF SEASIDE

From the first day of summer warmth, right through to the end of August, the first question I am asked by Italian friends and acquaintances is, 'Have you been (or are you going) to the sea today?' It's the Puglian equivalent of the British 'Hot enough for you?' – a friendly conversational gambit as the mercury rises. Nowhere in Puglia is far from the sea, except perhaps the very north, where you might have to drive for, oooh, almost an hour to reach the coast. I struggle to explain, even in this Covid-struck year, that I prefer the sandy beaches and rocky coves when they are quieter and the crowds have thinned out or disappeared completely.

In May, June and September, at the beginning and the end of the tourist season, the coastal sprawl of summer houses, cafés and restaurants provides us permanent residents with their happiest faces. This is the time to visit and to dip toes or more into the sea and search out the best seafood. In Torre Santa Sabina we sat on plastic chairs at a corner caff on the beachfront and lunched royally on grilled octopus rolls and a plate of perfect ozone-fresh sea urchins. In smarter Savelletri, we ate perfect *gamberi rossi crudi,* the sweetest, freshest raw prawns with no more than a drizzle of olive oil, followed by *frittura mista,* a fry-up of squid, prawns, cuttlefish and small fish, so crisped that you can eat tails and fins and bones and all.

And then the lights go out. From October, you can drive for kilometres through what suddenly looks like a devastated wasteland, devoid of human life. Turn off down the little alleys that lead to the shore and there's the magnificent coast, soft sandy beaches or rocky outcrops, howling winds, scrubby dunes, wheeling gulls, crashing waves. Of course, there are still pools of life in harbour towns and old fishing villages, where the inhabitants have slunk back into their normal humdrum tourist-free lives, but in between it's an elongated, coast-hugging ghost town.

A Swift Gallop Around Puglia's Coastlands

Let's start at the top right. Just a few miles after crossing the border with the Abruzzo, the Gargano Peninsula juts out into the Adriatic. The route to the tip of this spur introduces the driver to the appallingly pot-holed roads of much of Puglia. In mitigation, the sea views glimpsed through wooded slopes are spectacular. The most visited spot in the Gargano is not the beautiful harbour town of Vieste but San Giovanni Rotondo, home for fifty-two years to Padre Pio, Puglia's much venerated modern saint who died there in 1968.

Rushing onwards you soon come to the vast salt pans of Margherita di Savoia, the handsome cathedral town of Trani, then Bari, Puglia's capital. Holiday hot-spots abound as you head southwards, towns like Monopoli and Polignano that teeter right above the water, enchanting off-season, hell in August, then mile after mile of beaches, rocky inlets, nature reserves and small fishing hubs. I have a soft spot for the often-maligned city of Brindisi, where I first set foot on Italian soil when I was nineteen. Two stone columns at the harbour mark the end of the Appian Way, which led Roman merchants and armies to and from Rome.

One hundred and thirty-seven kilometres later, pausing only to admire Otranto, whose inhabitants were brutally massacred by Ottoman forces in 1480, you finally reach Puglia's tip, Santa Maria di Leuca, where the waters of the Adriatic and Ionian Seas wash into each other and the sunsets are breathtaking.

As you make your way northwards, up the Ionian coast, you notice a regular peppering of signs to Torre this and Torre that. There are more than 80 square towers squatting on Puglia's coastline. Some are crumbling, some are solid and handsome, some have small conurbations clustered around them, others stand proudly alone. The nervous Spanish rulers of the south of Italy built most of them three or four hundred years ago, defensive lookout posts to spot marauders and invaders before they got a chance to wreak damage.

The old cities of Gallipoli and Taranto both edge the blue sea. The first is beautifully preserved for the most part, thronged with tourists in the summer, delightful off-season. Elegant eateries and bars gaze out across the sea from the hexagonal walls. In Taranto's old town, you can buy a house for a single euro, so desperate are they to save it from total collapse. The huge polluting ex-Ilva steelworks belches fumes across the city that was once the most important of Magna Graecia.

Once away from the urban smog, Italy's instep curves round in a long sweep of sandy beach, fringed by forests of aromatic Aleppo pine, punctuated by the occasional holiday hub or marina, until it crosses the border into Basilicata just before the ancient ruins of Metaponto. *Arrivederci*, Puglia.

Fish Stews – a little bit of this and a little bit of that

Essentially, all Mediterranean fish stews are constructed along the same lines. The most elemental versions are the classic fishermen's stews, all cooked up in one large pan with ingredients that come easily to hand. At the other end of the scale are the grand restaurant versions, embellished with stocks and essences and items cooked separately, then reassembled. They all start with the same basics: very fresh, very local fish, shellfish, cephalopods and crustaceans in varying proportions, extra virgin olive oil, tomatoes, onions and/or garlic.

Puglia is no exception. Right the way around the long coastline you can dine on fish stew or soup of remarkable deliciousness. Each small town, or chef or cook or fisherman, has their own version, adding a splash of white wine here, chilli there, cuttlefish or squid, more expensive prawns or cheaper mussels. *Scorfano*, scorpion fish, is considered a masterful addition with its near gamey, satisfying flavour. Every *pescheria* (fishmonger) and supermarket sells mixed small bony fish, ideal for deep-frying which renders the bones crisp enough to eat, or to add an incredible flavour to soups and stews.

Not being a fisherman nor having a squad of keen young kitchen staff to do all the fiddly dirty work for me, I tend to hover somewhere between the two fish stew extremes, rather closer to the bottom end than the upper echelons. So, a slimmed-down roster of seafood, a one-pan, two-stage method, a gathering of some of my favourite Puglian flavourings, and the result, though I say it myself, is damn good.

Fish notes

To make a good fish stew you need a good fishmonger who sells pearly fresh, sweet-scented seafood. This is not a cheap option (not even if you buy straight from the harbour), so choose wisely to get the maximum flavour without breaking the bank. Mussels will add a sweet saltiness at a reasonable price. The same goes for squid. I reckon these two are essential. Prawns and langoustines are just fab, but costly. You can do without them. Mediterranean locals like to keep the little soup fish for themselves, so you'll need to replace them with a mix of medium-sized fish on the bone (e.g. sea bass, gurnard, red mullet, whiting) and some chunks of prime fleshy large fish such as cod or haddock.

Ciambotto

A local fish stew, with nods to the fishermen and cooks of Gallipoli, Porto Cesareo, Taranto and Bari.

Serves 4

600–800g mussels
2 medium-sized squid or cuttlefish
750g–1kg 'soup fish' and/or larger white fish
5 tablespoons extra virgin olive oil
1 large onion, sliced
4 cloves of garlic, chopped
2–4 red chillies, depending on strength, finely chopped
2 teaspoons fennel seeds
450g cherry tomatoes, halved or quartered depending on size
2 teaspoons dried oregano
3 tablespoons chopped flat-leaf parsley
1 glass white wine (around 150ml)
salt, if needed
slices of toasted bread rubbed with garlic

First prepare the mussels, squid and fish (see notes on pages 89–90) and set aside.

Put the oil, onion, garlic and chillies into a saucepan large enough to take all the ingredients. Place over a medium heat and cook gently, without browning, until tender. Add the fennel seeds and cook for a minute or so more. Tip in the cherry tomatoes, oregano and parsley. Simmer, stirring occasionally, for 10 minutes or so. Now, spread the pieces of fish on top, scatter over the squid strips, and top with the mussels. Pour over the glass of wine. Cover with a lid and cook for a further 10 minutes, until the mussels have all opened. Give the pan a little shake, then taste the juices to see if you need to add salt. Serve in bowls, with slices of garlicky toast tucked into each one.

Notes

Preparing the mussels: Tip the mussels into a sink and work through them methodically, pulling away the tough beard (or byssus as it is technically known) and scraping off barnacles. Rinse each one well under the cold tap. Discard any that are broken, or that don't close when rapped against the work surface. Rinse the whole lot one more time. And then rinse them again to get rid of as much sand and grit as possible.

Preparing the squid or cuttlefish: Begin by separating the head and tentacles from the body sac. Grasp the head and gently pull it away from the body, bringing with it the clear plasticky pen, and all the innards. Slice the tentacles off just above the eyes and reserve, then throw the rest of the gunk away. Now for the body – begin by pulling the wings away from the body (they detach surprisingly easily), then pull or rub away as much of the thin dark surface skin as you can, from both wings and body. Slit the squid sac open and scrape away any remaining jellyish innards. Cut the sac and wings into 1cm-wide strips. Rinse under the cold tap before using.

Preparing the fish: The golden rule here is to get your fishmonger to do most of the work for you. So, ask him or her to scale and clean all the fish and remove the fins and other pointy bony bits. When you get home, rinse the fish under the cold tap. Cut medium-sized fish into 1.5cm steaks, leaving the bone in situ (it adds to the flavour). Cut thicker fillets into decent-sized chunks (around 3cm across). Little fishes should just be beheaded.

If you have access to sustainably sourced soup fish, gut them and rinse in cold water. Tie them up in a square of muslin and add the parcel to the sauce 5 minutes before the rest of the seafood. Remove them before serving. This way you can get all the flavour without the pesky little bones.

Cozze Arraganate

Taranto-style Gratinated Mussels

Taranto was once a mighty sea power, due in part to its perfect sheltered Mare Piccolo, literally 'small sea' but actually an enormous lagoon, tucked behind the seafront city, with just one easily defended entrance from the Mare Grande, i.e. the city's stretch of the Ionian Sea. Once the Mare Piccolo provided a safe haven for Greek fleets; now it is home to the city's *mitilicoltura*, the mussel farms. Tarantinos love their mussels, cooking and eating them in dozens of ways. In 2019, Raffo, another big made-in-Taranto icon, produced a special edition beer with the motto 'Don't Touch my Cozza', as written, in Italenglish, emblazoned across the front.

Cozze arraganate is probably my favourite way of eating the local mussels, with its crisp drift of garlicky breadcrumbs and just a touch of white wine. Most recipes begin by saying that you should simply clean the mussels, then open them up with a narrow knife. As it turns out, this is not half as easy as it sounds, or as it looks on YouTube. This is frustrating, as it is undoubtedly true that the flesh stays sweeter and moister if you grill the mussels from raw. So, unless your fishmonger will do the job for you (unlikely, I'd have thought), or you are a glutton for punishment (my fingers were sore and red for days after my one and only attempt), I offer another way, which is nearly as good.

Serves 4 as a main course, 6–8 as a starter

700g mussels, cleaned (see page 89)
extra virgin olive oil
2 tablespoons white wine

For the crumbs
100g stale bread, torn into chunks, or dried breadcrumbs
1 large clove of garlic, roughly chopped
1 tablespoon roughly chopped flat-leaf parsley
30g freshly grated pecorino or Parmesan
salt and freshly ground black pepper
2 tablespoons extra virgin olive oil

For the crumbs, put the bread into a processor together with all the rest of the crumbs ingredients except the oil. Whiz together to make fine breadcrumbs. With the blades still running, trickle in the 2 tablespoons of olive oil. Set aside until needed.

Preheat the grill to its max. Spread the mussels out in a single layer in a roasting tin. Put them under the grill for just 2 minutes, which should be enough to spring them open. Find another wide, shallow, heatproof dish, big enough to take all the mussels in one layer. I usually use another roasting tin, but if you feel that's too slummy to put on your dinner table, make sure that whatever you use can take the heat of the grill. Coat the base lightly with olive oil.

As soon as the mussels are cool enough to handle, remove the upper shells. Arrange the mussels in their half shells in the oiled dish/tin. If not using immediately, cover with clingfilm and store in the fridge for up to 4 hours. If you are using a china or earthenware dish, be sure to bring it back to room temperature before sliding it under the grill, to prevent cracking.

Preheat the grill to maximum heat again if necessary. Dredge the crumbs mixture over the open mussels. Grill for 2–3 minutes, then carefully take from under the grill and drizzle the white wine over them. Return to the grill, and leave until the crumbs are golden brown and sizzling merrily. Let them cool for a couple of minutes, then serve.

Almost Japanese

There are very few things that I miss here: flaky sea salt, cheap paracetamol and ibuprofen and, most of all, Asian food. I miss that last-minute, empty-fridge, can't-be-arsed-to-cook dash for a quick Chinese or Thai or Indian. Eat-in, take-away, either would do nicely, thank you. Puglians are, on the whole, conservative eaters. If it ain't Italian food, it's just plain wrong. With one notable exception: Japanese. I can count at least four Japanese restaurants within a half hour's drive of my house.

I think it is fair enough to say that Japanese culture and Puglian culture do not have much of an overlap, but one communality stands out like a pickle in a pudding: a keen delight in eating raw fish. Naturally, the Japanese have transformed this into an art form, while the Pugliese like to keep things pure and simple without fuss or frills.

Pesce crudo is the first thing I order from a menu whenever I visit a seaside restaurant, despite the price. Perfect fresh fish, crustaceans and shellfish, all lustrous and plump and so very sexy. Oh, and cephalopods, in the form of translucent strips of squid or pearly white cuttlefish which is creamy smooth and tender. What a revelation that was. Best of all, though, are the *gambero rosso* and *gambero viola* from Gallipoli. I'm always taken by surprise at the exquisite sweet, delicate deliciousness of these red and violet prawns. They need no enhancement other than the few drops of extra virgin olive oil that will have been scattered over them before serving. A little finely chopped parsley doesn't go amiss, but that's more of a visual add-on.

The fanciest raw seafood gets in Puglia is when it is transformed into a simple *tartare*, very finely chopped tuna or prawns (usually), seasoned with olive oil, of course, salt, freshly ground black pepper and maybe a tiny squirt of lemon juice. A touch of lemon zest or finely chopped wild fennel herb or parsley is not unheard of but is far from essential. It's great as a starter and possibly even better as a sandwich filling.

Octopus

When my daughter, Florrie, made her first visit to Puglia, we stayed for a couple of hot nights in the Bari suburb of Santo Spirito. It was early June and spectacular lightning lit up the sky above the harbour arena, as the thunder roared. The rain passed us by, staying far out at sea in grey drapes. One tiny restaurant stood out from the rest, teeming with customers both inside and spilling out on to the pavement. Elbowing through the crammed bodies (this was way before social distancing) to the till to order took nerve and persistence, but paid dividends. It was here, at La Pucciaria, that I tasted my first grilled octopus *puccia,* essentially a hot smoky octopus *panino*.

Over the ensuing months I've realised, to my delight, that the octopus *puccia* or *rosetta* (a puffier, rather dull bread roll, enlivened only by its filling) is a commonplace snack, just one of the many pleasures of a trip to seaside, urban harbour, port or beach all around Puglia's long coastline. Octopus are plentiful. Apparently, stocks are booming, as the nascent octopedal survival rate is enhanced by the warming seas of climate change.

A few miles inland, however, and the octopus evaporates into thin air. No, let me rephrase that: it no longer appears on the menu of any decent snack bar and is rare on restaurant menus. It migrates to the occasional fish shop or market stand, as well as to supermarket fish counters and freezers. Every time I push my trolley past the tangle of frozen tentacles, I smile. It still seems so unexpected to a northern European like me.

From there, just a short hop to home kitchens and in particular to my kitchen.

I've been working, successfully, on eradicating a small niggly anxiety about cooking octopus. No idea why it lingers on, but I suspect I'm not alone. Is it just that it seems so alien a life form? All those legs, all those suckers. Will it be tough and chewy, will it crawl out of the pan to seek revenge before taking over the world? It suggests some kind of major kitchen undertaking, but in fact preparing and cooking octopus is so damn easy. So, just in case you're hesitating too, here's the how:

Choosing an octopus

Take what you can get, as long as it is pearly fresh and smells of no more than the purity of an ocean breeze on a remote beach, far from sewage outlets and rotting rubbish. Or as long as it is frozen. Freezing tenderises the flesh a little, so it's no second-rate option. Octopi come in many sizes. For grilling or barbecuing, it makes sense to opt for larger ones (1.5kg and upwards), so that the tentacles don't tumble down between the bars. Smaller ones cook more quickly. A 600g octopus will make a generous main course for 2 people, or for 3–4 if stretched with extra ingredients.

Will it be tough?

No. As long as you cook it long enough, and don't let the water/juices boil hard. A gentle simmer, or better still a few degrees under, is what it takes. Give it time, and it will become as tender as you want it.

As a teenager on my first trip to the Mediterranean, I noticed with horror a fisherman thrashing an octopus against a rock, over and over again to soften it. I wouldn't suggest emulating this at home unless you can hose down your entire kitchen afterwards. If your octopus is on the large side, you could thwack the tentacles with a meat mallet for a short while (good for releasing pent-up anger) to reduce the cooking time a little, but it's not an absolute necessity.

An easier option, if less therapeutic, would be to freeze it if it hasn't already been frozen and thawed. Again, not an absolute necessity.

Preparing it

With any luck the fishmonger will have done most of the work for you, but better to check thoroughly and remedy any oversights before cooking.

Let's begin with the anatomy. The eight tentacles meet in beautiful star formation, at the centre a small hole, housing the beak or mouth. Above this are the eyes, and flopping on top is the rest of the body, wrapped up in the fleshy mantle (often referred to as the hood by cooks).

First check that the mantle has been slit open and emptied. If not, you're going to have to do it yourself and although it's a bit icky, it can be done easily in seconds. The mantle itself is good to eat, so don't discard it with the gunk. If necessary, cut out the eyes in a neat wedge-shaped chunk. Now turn the octopus over to expose the star formation where the legs meet. Push the beak up through the central hole if it is still there and remove. Now give the whole thing a good rinse under the cold tap to flush out any lingering sandy grit. Done.

Cooking options

All octopus recipes begin with slow, gentle simmering or braising (as in the *pignata* recipe on page 102), either whole or in pieces. For salads, grilling or barbecuing, cook the beast whole in a large pan of simmering water. You can just plop the whole octopus into the water, but if you want the tentacles to curl into the cutest spiralled ringlets, dunk it in and out a few times first.

For up to 2 kilos weight of octopus, put the pot of water on the heat and add a couple of generous pinches of salt (not too much at this point, as octopus can be quite salty) and some or all of the following:

juice of ½ a lemon, and the squeezed half lemon itself
1 small onion, quartered
1 carrot, cut into chunks
1 stem of celery, thickly sliced
2 bay leaves
a few sprigs of flat-leaf parsley or coriander
a few sprigs of thyme
a few sprigs of fennel or dill

Heat until the surface of the water is trembling, but not quite hitting a rolling boil. Grasp the octopus by the fleshiest bit and dangle a couple of centimetres of the legs into the hot water, hold for 10 seconds, then lift out. This starts the tentacles curling. Repeat three more times, lowering the tentacles a little more each time. Now submerge the whole octopus in the water.

Leave to cook gently, at a bare simmer, for anything from 30 minutes to 2 hours depending on the size of the octopus. Top up the water levels occasionally so that the octopus remains submerged. Test every once in a while by pushing a cocktail stick into the thickest parts of the flesh. When it slides in sweetly and easily, lift out the octopus and do whatever comes next in the recipe.

A final note

Get the octopus into its marinade/dressing while still warm, so that it absorbs more of the flavours.

Insalata di Polpo al Finocchio e Arancia

Octopus, Fennel and Orange Salad

Serves 6 as a starter, 4 as part of a light lunch

600–800g octopus, cleaned and cooked

For the salad
juice of ½–1 lemon
4 tablespoons extra virgin olive oil
2 cloves of garlic, crushed
salt and freshly ground black pepper
2 heaped tablespoons freshly chopped flat-leaf parsley
1 head of fennel, trimmed, quartered and cut into thin slices
1 orange, peeled and cut into chunks
80–90g black olives, stoned if you are feeling patient

As soon as the octopus is cooked, hoick it out of the pan and cut it into bite-sized pieces. Toss with the juice of half a lemon, the olive oil, garlic, salt and lots of freshly ground black pepper. Leave to cool.

Shortly before serving, mix with the remaining ingredients, taste and adjust the seasoning (you'll probably need to add more lemon juice and salt), and serve at room temperature.

Pugliese Octopus Salad

Cook a couple of potatoes, peeled and cut into 2.5cm chunks, in with the octopus for the last 15 minutes or so of its cooking time. Cut up the octopus, and while the potatoes and octopus are still warm, toss them with lemon juice, olive oil, salt and freshly ground black pepper and leave to cool. Finally, toss with halved cherry tomatoes, capers, black olives and rocket.

Serve at room temperature.

Polpo alla Pignata

Slow-braised Octopus

It was a dark and stormy night (no, it really was) and I was marooned in pre-season Porto Cesareo on the Ionian coast. I picked a restaurant at random because it looked warm and cosy and not too pretentious. It was here that I first tasted *polpo alla pignata*, cooked long and slow in a sealed pot. It came unadorned, just a salad on the side and some so-so bread to mop the plate clean. Bloody marvellous.

As it turns out, this is one of the easiest and best ways of cooking octopus in the colder months. The key is to seal all the steam and flavour hermetically into the pot so that nothing is lost, and to keep the heat gentle and unaggressive throughout. An earthenware pot is ideal, but failing that a heavy casserole dish will do fine. Do not skimp on the olive oil. And do skin the tomatoes if using fresh ones, so that the flesh can melt down to create the sublime sauce.

Serves 4

1 or 2 octopus, weighing about 800g altogether, cleaned
5 tablespoons extra virgin olive oil
1 onion, sliced
4 cloves of garlic, chopped
1 x 400g tin of chopped tomatoes, or 400g fresh tomatoes, skinned and roughly chopped
a good handful of flat-leaf parsley, chopped
4 sprigs of fennel, chopped
1 bay leaf
lots of freshly ground black pepper

Rinse the octopus under the cold tap. Cut the tentacles into 2–3cm lengths. Cut the hood into similar-sized pieces.

Put the oil, onion and garlic into a flameproof casserole dish with a lid. Set over a moderate heat. Once the oil is hot, fry for a few minutes until the onion wilts. Now add all the remaining ingredients including the octopus. Don't add any salt yet – octopus can be quite salty. Stir and heat through. Turn the heat down low. Lay a double layer of foil over the top and clamp the lid on firmly. The idea is to seal in all the juices, so if there is a steam hole in the lid, make sure that is covered as well. Leave to cook gently for 1½–2 hours (depending on the size of the octopuses), stirring occasionally, until the octopus is as tender as butter. If it threatens to dry and catch, add a splash or two of water, then turn the heat lower and make sure the seal is as tight as can be. Taste and adjust the seasoning, adding salt if needed. Serve as it is or tossed with pasta, or, possibly best of all, on a pile of steaming hot polenta.

Saucier Braised Octopus

If you fancy serving the octopus in traditional two-course style, double the amount of tomato to 2 tins of chopped tomatoes or use 800ml of passata. Forget about fresh tomatoes unless you happen to have an excess to use up. Stew just as before in the *pignata* recipe on page 102, long and slow and lovingly until the octopus is super-tender. Fish the bits of octopus out and keep warm, or reheat in a minimal amount of sauce later.

Toss the rest of the sauce into spaghetti or tagliatelle to serve as a *primo piatto*, first course, followed by the octopus itself with fresh greens of some sort or another.

Mex-Italian Grilled Octopus

I love Puglian grilled octopus and eat it whenever I can, but I have to admit that the best grilled octopus I've ever eaten was in the backstreets of Tulum in Mexico. So in homage to that, I bathe my Italian octopus in a marinade enlivened with smoky chipotle chillies and lots of lime, before it goes over the coals. It's a good marriage, improved even more with a chipotle basil mayonnaise on the plate.

Serves 4

1 x 800g–1kg octopus, cooked

For the marinade
4 dried chipotle chillies
½ a small onion, sliced
2 medium-sized tomatoes
2 cloves of garlic
salt
juice of 1 lime
a handful of basil leaves
3 tablespoons extra virgin olive oil

For the chipotle basil mayonnaise
1 egg
salt and freshly ground black pepper
1 tablespoon very hot water
juice of 1 lime
2 cloves of garlic, roughly chopped
290ml sunflower oil

50ml extra virgin olive oil
a small handful of basil leaves

Make the marinade while the octopus is cooking.

Put the chipotle chillies, onion, tomatoes and garlic cloves into a saucepan and cover with water. Bring to the boil and simmer for 7 minutes. Take out the tomatoes, and leave the rest to carry on simmering until the chipotles, onion and garlic are soft – another 15 minutes or so. Take off the heat. Drain, RESERVING THE COOKING WATER. Remove the chipotle stalks and deseed the chillies. Skin the tomatoes. Pile the tomatoes, chipotles, onion, garlic and a little salt into a food processor or liquidiser and blend to a thick purée, adding a spoonful or two of the reserved cooking water if needed. Set aside 2 tablespoons of the chipotle purée. Add the lime juice, basil, oil and a little salt to what's left in the processor and whiz up again.

As soon as the octopus is cooked, divide the main clump of tentacles into the 8 separate legs, and cut the hood in half. Mix with the marinade. Leave to cool and marinate for at least 2 hours, or better still overnight (in the fridge).

While the octopus is marinating, make the chipotle basil mayonnaise. Break the egg into the food processor or liquidiser and add a few generous pinches of salt. Whiz briefly to mix, then with the motor still running, add the hot water. Add the lime juice and garlic, then, still with the blades whizzing round, trickle in the sunflower oil in a slow, steady stream, followed by the olive oil. Now add the reserved chipotle purée and the basil leaves. Whiz it all up until smooth. Taste and adjust the seasonings. Done. Store, covered, in the fridge until needed.

Preheat the grill/griddle pan/barbecue thoroughly. Shake the marinade off the octopus, then cook over a high heat for 5–10 minutes, until hot and patched with brown. Serve immediately with the chipotle basil mayo.

Tiella Foggiana

Salt Cod, Potato and Rice Gratin

Italy (and before it, the principalities and kingdoms that jostled together on the pre-Italian peninsula) is a country that has survived on carbs of one sort or another for centuries. Bread, pasta, pulses, pies, rice and, to a lesser extent, potatoes have kept the poor alive and working. Puglia is a shining beacon of carbiness, and the *tiella* stands proudly at the forefront, a glorious gratin of potatoes and rice, uplifted with tomatoes, onions and mussels (in Bari and around the coast), or salt cod (in Foggia and inland).

The Barese version is an odd dish, with mussels in their half shell buried under the potatoes and rice. The taste is good, but by the time it emerges from the oven, the mussels themselves have had all their sweetness baked out of them and are mere shadows of their former selves. In restaurants it is inevitably reheated, which doesn't improve matters. This Foggia *tiella*, on the other hand, would definitely make it into my top ten Pugliese dishes. The rich, tantalising smell as it emerges from the oven is irresistible. And it reheats pretty well, too.

Here I can buy ready-to-go desalted *baccalà* (salt cod) from the *pescheria* or in the supermarket. It is ferociously expensive, so a recipe like this, that exploits a small amount by loading up the carbs, is most welcome. If you can only find dried salt cod, you will have to start desalting it 2 days in advance.

Serves 6

330g dried salt cod, desalted, or 400g soaked, desalted salt cod (see note on page 110)
2 red onions, chopped
350g tomatoes or cherry tomatoes, chopped
4 cloves of garlic, finely chopped
3 tablespoons chopped flat-leaf parsley
2 tablespoons capers, well-rinsed if salted
8 tablespoons extra virgin olive oil
800g potatoes, peeled and very thinly sliced
salt and freshly ground black pepper
150g rice (long-grain or risotto rice)
100g freshly grated pecorino or Parmesan

Preheat the oven to 220°C/200°C fan/gas 7.

Remove the skin and any bones from the salt cod, then cut it into 1.5cm chunks.

Find a circular baking dish roughly 24–26cm in diameter. Mix the onions, tomatoes, garlic, parsley, capers and olive oil in a bowl. Spread a quarter of this mixture over the base of the baking dish. Now arrange one third of the potatoes over this. Season with salt and pepper. Scatter half the salt cod on top, followed by another quarter of the onion, tomato and parsley mixture. And then scatter over half the rice and a quarter of the cheese.

Repeat these layers one more time. Cover with the remaining third of the potatoes, and over that the last of the tomato mixture. Season with salt and pepper. Now the important bit. Slowly pour near-boiling water down the sides of the dish, until the level rises to just a millimetre or two below the top layer of potatoes. Shake the dish gently to distribute the water more evenly. Finish by dredging the top with the last of the cheese.

Cover with foil and bake for 45 minutes. Uncover and bake for a further 45 minutes, until the water is virtually all absorbed, and a knife plunged down into the *tiella* slides sweetly through the potatoes and rice without resistance. If it threatens to burn towards the end of the cooking time, re-cover loosely with foil.

Let it cool for 5–10 minutes (or longer – it tastes just as good, if not better, when warm), then dig in.

Note

To desalt salt cod: It helps if you start with good-quality salt cod, by which I mean a decent chunky piece, say 1–2cm thick. It should be creamy white, not nicotine-yellow. Place the salt cod in a shallow bowl or plastic box. Pour in enough cold water to cover, then cover with a beeswax cloth, clingfilm or a lid and leave to soak in the fridge for 48 hours, changing the water at least twice a day. Taste a little corner of the fish to see how it's doing. If it is still overly salty, pour over more cold water and leave for a few more hours. Drain before using.

Tagliata di Tonno

Seared Tuna and Rocket Salad

When I ordered a *tagliata* of tuna in a tiny three-table restaurant, the waiter (and husband of the cook in the kitchen, and owner and probably bottlewasher, too) asked rather nervously whether I wanted cheese on it. I felt his anxiety. Tuna *tagliata* is a take on the better-known steak *tagliata,* a dish of thinly sliced seared steak served on a bed of rocket and tomato and, most importantly, finished with a generous flurry of Parmesan or pecorino shavings. And there's the rub – in Italy it is a cardinal sin to ask for grated cheese of any sort to sprinkle over your seafood spaghetti, or any other kind of fish. The cheese masks the delicate flavour of the fish and is therefore an insult, as it implies that you think the fish is not as fresh as it should be.

The Pugliese are not averse to a spot of rule-breaking, even in the kitchen. Cheese creeps into more than a few of its cherished local fish recipes, bringing an umami lift to other flavours without overwhelming. There is cheese in the crisp breadcrumb topping of Taranto's *cozze arraganate* (see page 91), and in Foggia's *tiella* of salt cod (see page 108). Here, it marries well with the full meaty flavour of seared tuna. So, Signor WaiterHusbandOwnerBottlewasher, the answer is, 'Yes, I definitely do want cheese on my tuna *tagliata.* And a pile of chips or sautéd potatoes to go with it, please.'

Serves 2

2 good handfuls of rocket
1 medium-sized juicy tomato, roughly chunked, or 250g cherry tomatoes, halved

a small handful of basil
3 tablespoons balsamic vinegar
1 or 2 tuna steaks (350–400g total weight), cut about 2.5cm thick
2–3 tablespoons extra virgin olive oil, plus extra for brushing
a few squeezes of lemon juice
salt and freshly ground black pepper
1 heaped teaspoon capers, rinsed if salted
30g Parmesan shavings

Start by spreading your rocket out on a serving plate, or individual plates, then scatter the tomato(es) and basil over it. Mix the balsamic vinegar with 2 tablespoons of cold water.

Put a heavy-based frying pan or flat griddle (annoyingly, ridgy ones won't work here – you'll lose most of the sauce) over a high heat. Let it get outrageously hot. Turn on your extractor fan if you have one. Pat the tuna steak(s) dry with kitchen paper, then brush lightly with a little olive oil on both sides. Lay them in the pan and sear them for 1 minute on each side. Do not fiddle with them. Transfer them to a chopping board. Turn the heat off under the pan, then tip in the balsamic vinegar and water mix. While it bubbles down, quickly season the tuna with a squeeze or two of lemon juice and salt and pepper.

You'll probably need to turn the heat back on under the pan to finish the sauce. As soon as the balsamic juices have sizzled down to around 2 tablespoonfuls, add the capers, measured olive oil, salt and pepper. Stir for a few seconds until hot, hot, hot. Turn off the heat. With a very sharp knife, slice the tuna and arrange on top of the rocket and tomato(es). Drizzle over the hot dressing, and scatter over the Parmesan shavings. Eat.

Pesce all'Acqua Pazza

Fish in Crazy Water

This is a Neapolitan summer dish, but too good not to enjoy here in Puglia where the fish is so fresh and sparkling. *Acqua pazza* means crazy water, describing the scary bubbling of the hot-as-hell oil, when the water is poured in.

I'm always tempted to add a few extra tomatoes, but it's a mistake. This is not fried fish in tomato sauce, but fried and braised fish in a broth that catches the essential flavours of olive oil and tomato in a totally different manner. Nor, for that matter, should you reduce the quantity of oil. It is the second most important element of the dish, after the fish itself.

Serves 4

2 whole sea bream, sea bass or bream, scaled, de-finned, trimmed and cleaned
150ml extra virgin olive oil
4 cloves of garlic, sliced or roughly chopped
1 or 2 red chilli(es), finely chopped, seeds and all
16 cherry tomatoes (or 20 if they are particularly small), quartered
a handful of black olives (optional)
a major handful of basil leaves, roughly torn up
salt
200ml water (or white wine if there is some hanging around)

Make a couple of diagonal slashes across the thickest part of each fish, on each side, so that they cook evenly.

Heat the olive oil in a large, heavy-based, deep frying pan over a high heat. Add the fish – be prepared, as it will sizzle madly. After a minute or so, scatter over the garlic, chilli(es), tomatoes, olives, basil and salt. Turn the fish and fry for a minute or so, making sure the olive oil heats right up again.

Now for the *acqua pazza* part. Pour in a slurp of the water and listen to the craziness. Now add the rest of the water. Once all is simmering together nicely, turn the heat down a tad and cook for another 6–10 minutes, turning the fish once, until cooked through.

Transfer the fish to a serving dish, then boil the juices in the pan down a little more to concentrate the flavours. Taste and adjust the seasoning, then pour over the fish. It's ready to serve.

4

WOOD-FIRED OVENS

Bread – the Good, the Bad and the Ugly, but mostly the Good

I've long harboured a niggling suspicion that bread is Italy's culinary Achilles heel. To be sure there are some great Italian breads, and not just those international jet-setters ciabatta (invented in 1982), focaccia and pizza (both of which have long histories). Put these aside, and the vast majority of the bread sold in Italy is either heavy, stodgy doorstops or soft, tasteless sponges with a tough outer crust. An odd state of affairs for a country that takes such pride in its food.

And yet, and yet, and yet . . . bread is perhaps as important, if not more important, a part of the daily diet as pasta here in Puglia. If you go back to the early twentieth century, there was rioting in the streets when bread prices went up. Bread was the stomach filler of the poor, eaten with an onion or tomato as '*companatico*' to add flavour. And when you couldn't afford wheat bread, it was chestnut flour or bean flour bread or polenta. Puglian cooking is awash with recipes that include breadcrumbs or stale bread soaked in water or milk to soften it. Not a crumb is ever allowed to go to waste, and those crumbs taste so much better in cheesey *polpette di pane* (see page 167) or toasted to a crisp over salty sweet mussels (*cozze arraganate*, see page 91).

My enthusiasm when I first saw potato bread for sale in the little bakery down the Corso Verdi was soon dampened. It wasn't the fabulously delicious potato and rosemary sourdough breads I've enjoyed back in the UK. Slicing the solid bread torpedo near blunted the knife. The dough was dense and cakey, with little knobbles of barely cooked potato here and there. In the end I processed it to breadcrumbs and hid them in the freezer to await a greater purpose.

I blame the leaden loaves not on the bakers per se, but on the flour. Italian wheat flours, for the most part, have less protein in them than wheat flours milled from grain grown in cooler climates. That means less gluten, less elasticity, less bounce. It takes a skilled baker to create a good loaf with it. My own baking skills have been severely challenged and found wanting. The focaccia that I made so confidently back in the UK with regular strong bread flour has failed spectacularly here on several occasions, emerging from the oven flaccid and damp, fit only for the bin. Oh, the shame . . .

Galloping in to the rescue comes the wonderful durum wheat, which is ground down into semolina flour, as strong as iron. The best bread and the best pasta are made with durum wheat. I just love it, and I can't fathom why it is so difficult to find outside Italy. Down here in Italy's heel there's one variety that is prized above all, Senatore Cappelli. It was developed in the early years of the twentieth century, in Foggia in the north of Puglia, and remains a golden wonder. Now, whenever I want to make bread my hand reaches automatically for the Senator's flour.

Pane di Altamura

Luckily for me, Puglia has produced one of the handful of great Italian breads. This one hasn't broken out into world-wide fame and is probably all the better for it. Since 2003 the golden-crumbed *pane di Altamura* has been fiercely protected by a PDO (Protected Designation of Origin), which means it can only be made in the area around the town of Altamura, up on the Murgia plains in the north of the region, with the right ingredients and by the right method. This means that even when it is made in a moderately large-scale bakery, then packed in plastic bags and sent down to my local supermarket, it is still in terrific form.

Better still, of course, is the bread that comes from the small, ultra-traditional bakers in the town itself. My last exploratory outing before the hammer of Covid-19 lockdown fell upon us was to Altamura and its neighbour Gravina, which also falls in the PDO delineated bread region. Altamura is as beautiful as so many of the towns here, with its twisting maze of medieval streets that, if you are lucky, open out on to the central Corso Federico II di Svevia. Naturally, I got extremely, though happily, lost and ended up back on the outskirts, just a few hundred yards from where I'd parked the car.

This Corso Federico is Altamura's axle, a long, wide, mostly pedestrian street around which the entire town spins. Here are the grandest *palazzi*, the chicest shops and cafés, and at the very centre a stately cathedral guarded by two stone lions, one of which looks painfully mournful. Among the Cattedrale di Santa Maria Assunta's various claims to fame, the outstanding one is that it is the first and only cathedral in Puglia to be built by the Holy Roman Emperor Frederick II, who had a lifelong passion for the region. When he died in 1250 he left behind him a vast quantity of magnificent palaces and fortifications, many of which still stand to this day. He spent much of his life fighting alternately with or against the Pope, which may have contributed to his lack of enthusiasm for piling good money into ecclesiastical construction.

Having finally located and admired the cathedral, it was only a short hop around a couple more corners, past a nunnery, a chapel and a garage with cars and mechanics spilling out on to the street, to what claims to be the oldest bakery in town. The Forno Santa Chiara is tiny, pushed unceremoniously into a corner of a small piazza, rough around the edges. There's a wall of logs next to the red-hot mouth of the ancient bread oven, which is almost as big as the shop itself. Its stone-paved floor is pitted and uneven and right at the back there is a cluster of loaves shimmering in the heat.

Piled up on racks on shelves by the counter, massive crusty loaves crackle as they cool. There's a wooden trestle table in the centre of the room, with tomato and olive topped *focacce* and wheels of *calzoni farciti*, stuffed *focacce* and pies. It does indeed look, smell and sound like a bakery that's changed little in the past 600 years, apart from a few modern gadgets like electricity, contactless payment and the floury radio blaring out Dance Monkey from a gloomy corner. I leave with a 2-kilo loaf weighting my bag, still warm and sweet-scented, and a wedge of what turns out to be one of the most delicious pies I've tasted in a long while, with a crumbling, deep brown oily pastry and a filling of soft, caramelised onion flecked with salami. A few days later, President Giuseppe Conte announced the first Italian lockdown. My first quarantine mission, I decided, was to recreate them both, to the best of my ability, in my own kitchen. It was going to be a long time before I could return to Altamura for second helpings.

Recipe notes

Semolina FLOUR is essential. This is a fine-milled version of semolina, used not only for bread but also for most commercial pasta. It is not the same as the semolina sold in supermarkets, the stuff of dreaded school puddings of old, nor is it the same as 00 pasta flour. Semolina is durum wheat. Durum wheat is a high-protein über-strong category of wheat. In Italy it is sold as *semola rimacinata di grano duro* – remilled hard-wheat semolina. So many names, so confusing. Track it down in Italian delis or buy it online.

Semolina flour is a joy for breadmaking. It produces the most beautiful primrose-yellow crumb, with plenty of flavour. As you knead the dough, all that protein softens easily into bouncy gluten, to give a substantial tender texture to the finished loaf. Very satisfying all round.

A *biga* is what is known in baker's jargon as a preferment. I used to think that a preferment was just whatever method you happened to prefer, but there's more to it than that. It's really a prequel to the main breadmaking session (i.e. the ferment), where all the ingredients are mixed together and kneaded, shaped, proved and baked. Like any decent film prequel, it adds extra depth and richness, and a more substantial texture.

An Italian *biga* is a mix of flour, water and a small amount of yeast that's left alone for anything from 12 to 24 hours. In this time the yeast multiplies and gains strength from the flour, developing flavour and structure. The point is that it makes a really good loaf of bread.

When you use a *biga*, you need far less yeast than for a standard loaf. In this case, a single 7g sachet of fast-action dried yeast is all you need for 1kg of flour. With fresh yeast, it's a mere 15g.

Altamura-style Bread

Makes 1 large loaf

For the biga *(Day 1)*
500g semolina flour (not pudding semolina)
5g fresh yeast or 2g fast-action dried yeast
350ml warm water

For the loaf (Day 2)
500g semolina flour (as above), plus extra for dusting
10g fresh yeast or 5g fast-action dried yeast
250ml warm water
5g malt, dark muscovado sugar or honey
20g salt

Day 1

Start the *biga*: put the Day 1 batch of flour into a large bowl. If using fresh yeast, crumble it into a small bowl and add a couple of spoonfuls of the warm water. Mash to a cream, then work in a splash or two more water. Add to the flour together with the remaining water, or add the dried yeast directly to the flour along with all the water. Mix well, then cover with a large beeswax cloth, or clingfilm, or slide into a plastic bag and tuck the ends underneath. Leave at room temperature for 16–20 hours.

Day 2

Now the loaf: put the Day 2 batch of flour into a large bowl. If using fresh yeast, crumble and cream with a little warm water as before. Add to the flour together with the remaining water, or if using dried yeast, add directly to the flour with the water. Uncover your *biga*, which should be merrily pitted with bubbles, and scrape that into the bowl as well. Add the malt, muscovado sugar or honey and the salt and mix the whole lot together to form a slightly sticky dough.

Dust the work surface lightly with more semolina flour and while you are at it, dust a baking sheet generously with semolina flour as well. Turn the dough out on to the work surface. Knead energetically for around 10 minutes, until the dough is smooth and elastic. Form into a tubby, oval loaf-shape. Transfer to the baking sheet. Sprinkle the top with a little more semolina flour (to stop the covering sticking). Cover loosely with a beeswax cloth or clingfilm, or slide sheet and loaf into a plastic bag, puffing it up so that there's room for the loaf to expand. Set aside at room temperature to rise until almost doubled in volume – this will take a good 2–3 hours, or possibly longer in a cool room.

Preheat the oven to 220°C/200°C fan/gas 7. Carefully remove the covering from the loaf. With a very sharp knife or craft-knife, make two long slashes down the length of the loaf. Bake for 50 minutes or so, until richly browned. Tap the base and see if it sounds hollow. If it thuds in a dull, heavy way, pop it back on the baking sheet, butt upwards, and give it another 10 minutes in the oven.

Leave to cool on a wire rack for as long as you can resist it.

Two *Focacce*

I discovered the beauty of focaccia and Siena in the same week, some forty years ago. Back then, focaccia was not a thing in the UK. Now, I'm tempted to argue that it still isn't, not truly, or at best only in a limited fashion. I remember the thrill of taking my brown-paper-wrapped parcel, oil seeping through in darker patches here and there, from the small backstreet *negozio di alimentari* (family-run deli) to the sloping shell of Siena's Piazza del Campo.

Then came a small moment of perfection, never forgotten. The taste of freshly baked focaccia, filled with salty *prosciutto crudo*, sweet tomato, milky mozzarella, my butt warmed by the red brick of the piazza floor, gazing at one of the most beautiful city squares in the world. I was at an age when the world was opening up for me, when freedom, independence and discovery fired up all my senses. I had fallen in love with Italy, a love that has endured for all of my adult life, eclipsed only by the profound love I have for my children.

As with all love affairs, time and experience change how we perceive our beloved. Italy is far, far from perfect. Behind the beautiful façade there lie centuries of pain and corruption. Racism, sexism and discrimination are widespread. Despite this it is a land of generosity and human warmth. My downstairs neighbour Maria shouts up to me, *'Sofia, Sofia, scendi, scendi!'* Come down, come down. I've learned to obey without hesitation, knowing that this heralds a plate of something delicious about to be thrust into my hand.

One lockdown Saturday I was invited to join her and her son and daughter-in-law (we'd formed our own interhousehold bubble) at her orchard plot a few miles from town. Focaccia day. A big treat for us all. The dough, slicked with olive oil, had been rising slowly overnight. The first task that morning was to light the fire in the old bread oven, stoking it with this year's olive prunings and last year's seasoned logs. By the time the heat reached fever pitch, her focaccia was ready to roast. It was nothing like the Sienese focaccia I'd tucked into decades before.

For a start, the dough was softened with cooked potato. Slabs of dough were rolled out thin, then sandwiched together with tomato, mozzarella and pungent *ricotta forte*, before sliding on to the screamingly hot stone tiles of the oven. Despite the filling it still emerged thinner than its northern predecessor, a little charred underneath, a whiff of smoke from the wood. This filled focaccia is much loved here, unlike the guacamole I brought with me to go with it. Maria took one suspicious teaspoonful and rejected it out of hand. I, on the other hand, tucked into her focaccia with relish.

Though there are any number of variations on focaccia throughout Italy, the common element is that they are all hearth breads. In other words, they are all relatively thin, and cook quickly in the fierce heat of a wood-fired oven at its hottest, so don't be afraid to turn your oven up high. By the time the *focacce* are done, the wood-fired oven has cooled just enough to take larger loaves without risk of burning.

Focaccia Barese

The old town of Bari is well-stocked with shops, bakers and cafés offering the city's rich, oily version of focaccia, studded with jagged ripped tomatoes and green olives. *Origano selvatico*, intensely aromatic dried wild oregano from the countryside, adds the defining touch. On my first trip to the city, I spot *focaccia barese* in the renowned Panificio Fiore, near the Basilica San Nicola, at Panificio Violante, on the long counter of Salumeria Da Nino, and then again and again and again, wherever I look, but my first bite was from a hastily bought slice of focaccia snatched as I queued to board a plane back to the UK. Probably the best airport food ever.

Makes 1 focaccia, serving anything from 6 to 12 depending on circumstance

either:
550g semolina flour (not pudding semolina)
or:
350g strong white bread flour and 200g pudding semolina (which works fine here)
225g mashed potato
1 x 7g sachet of fast-action dried yeast or 15g fresh yeast (crumbled)
10g salt
4–5 tablespoons extra virgin olive oil

To finish
more extra virgin olive oil
120g or so small tomatoes or cherry tomatoes
green olives, stoned and roughly halved
dried oregano

Mix the flour, semolina, mashed potato, yeast, salt, olive oil and enough water (around 350–400ml) to make a really soft, sticky dough. The dough will be too damp to knead in the conventional way, so keep it in the bowl and slap it about, stretching it as much as you can, and then scooping around the bowl, pulling it up and working it some more. Keep going for some 5–10 minutes. It's a sticky business, but once you've got the hang of it, strangely satisfying.

Cover the bowl with a beeswax cloth, clingfilm, or with a tea towel wrung out in water. Leave for an hour or so at room temperature, until the dough is well risen. Pour at least another 3 tablespoons of olive oil into a 28–30cm diameter cake tin and swirl it around to cover the sides. Scoop the dough into the tin, and push and spread it out to fill evenly. Cover again and leave to rise until it fills the tin.

Preheat the oven to 220°C/200°C fan/gas 7.

Now take a tomato at a time and rip it apart with your fingers, allowing the juice to rain down on the surface of the focaccia, then dot the flesh of the tomatoes generously on the dough. Sprinkle with olives, add a good drizzle of olive oil and finish with a scattering of salt and lots of oregano. Bake for around 25 minutes, until browned and until you can't resist the aroma any longer. Patience. Let your *focaccia barese* cool until just bearable to handle, then carefully lever it out of the tin and transfer to a wire rack. Eat now or save for later. All that oil means it will keep for several days in an airtight container, if necessary.

Focaccia con Patate e Rosmarino

Potato and Rosemary Focaccia

My last stop when I go to the Saturday market is always at the excellent Forno di San Lorenzo bakery. It's the smartest, most modern and best bakery in town. The female waiting staff are all cheerily chic with bright red lipstick and flat caps, chatting loudly to customers and bakers, calling everyone *cara*, dear, as they hurtle from one end of the counter to the other. I buy their delicious seedy bread and a treat for my lunch. I need a treat after hauling all the fruit and veg back up the steep hill to my house. That treat is usually a fat wedge of their potato focaccia, still warm from the oven. It's good on its own, split and filled with tomato and spicy hot 'nduja sausage, or dipped into a bowl of soup to banish the damp chill of winter.

The challenge with this particular focaccia is getting both potatoes and bread dough cooked through in sync. Start with an extremely hot oven to get the dough going, then turn it down to finish cooking the potatoes at a more modest temperature.

Makes a decent-sized focaccia, enough for 6–8 substantial portions, or 12 smaller cubes

650g strong white bread flour
2 teaspoons salt
3 tablespoons extra virgin olive oil, plus extra for oiling the dish and hands
400–425ml lukewarm water
15g fresh yeast or 1 x 7g sachet of fast-action dried yeast

To top
1 potato, weighing somewhere between 250g and 300g
1 tablespoon extra virgin olive oil
leaves from 1 sprig of rosemary
flaky salt

Smear a tablespoon of olive oil around a 28cm x 30cm (or thereabouts) roasting tin. Now for the dough. If you have a sturdy stand mixer you can do the whole lot in that, including kneading. Otherwise, arm yourself with a large bowl and flex your arm muscles.

With fresh yeast: put the flour into a big bowl with the salt and make a well in the centre. Spoon in the olive oil and about a quarter of the warm water. Crumble in the yeast and smoosh it up with your fingers to dissolve it into the water. Now add most of the remaining water and mix to a ridiculously soft and sticky dough that verges on sloppy. Do not panic.

With dried yeast: put the flour, salt, yeast and oil into the bowl, then add most of the water to produce a ridiculously soft dough (see fresh yeast method).

Begin to knead: scoop your hand down and around the side of the dough and stretch up a handful of damp mixture, then slap it back over the remaining dough. Turn the bowl slightly and repeat. Keep doing the same thing for 10 minutes – you'll soon develop an amiable rhythm. Little by little, the dough will become smoothly elastic and stretchy. Now scrape it out into the oiled roasting tin. Get as much as you can off your hands and add that, too. Wash your hands, then smear a little more oil over your fingers and palms. Press and push and smooth the dough down to cover the base. Cover loosely with a beeswax cloth if you have one, or slide the tin into a plastic bag, tucking the ends underneath. Leave in a warm place until at least doubled in volume.

Preheat the oven to 250°C/230°C fan/gas 9.

Prepare the topping: peel the potato. Cut into slices no more than 2mm thick. Mix with the tablespoon of olive oil and the rosemary leaves. Once the dough has risen, lay the potato slices gently on top, complete with clingy rosemary leaves, overlapping them just a little, like the tiles of a roof. You may not need them all, but make sure there are plenty of rosemary leaves among them. Sprinkle with flaky salt. Bake for 15 minutes, then lower the temperature to 200°C/180°C fan/gas 6 and continue baking for another 20–30 minutes. Stick the point of a knife into one or two of the potatoes to check that they are cooked through. Cool for a few minutes in the tin, then transfer to a wire rack.

Eat warm or at room temperature.

Pitta di Cipolle

Caramelised Onion Pie

This is as close as I can get to the remarkable onion pie I bought in Altamura. It will never be as good without the heat and smoke of the ancient wood-fired oven, but it comes somewhere near. Making a dough with olive oil and wine is a classic round here – *taralli*, the little crisp dough rings eaten as a snack with drinks, are another fine example.

Serves 6

For the pastry
400g plain flour
100ml extra virgin olive oil
100ml dry white wine
1 egg, lightly beaten
2 good pinches of salt
to glaze: 1 egg, lightly beaten

For the filling
1kg onions, halved and thinly sliced
4–5 tablespoons extra virgin olive oil
10 cherry tomatoes, quartered
either:
70g Italian salami, diced
or:
80–90g Gorgonzola dolce or piccante, diced small if not too gooey
salt and freshly ground black pepper

First get the filling going. Put the onions and the oil into a medium-sized saucepan, preferably with a heavy base. Set over a low heat, cover and let the onions stew gently in their own juices and the oil for 20–30 minutes, until they are beautifully floppy and soft. Give them a stir once in a while as they cook. Now stir in the tomatoes, and the salami, if using, and cook, uncovered, for another 5–10 minutes, stirring frequently, until the tomatoes have softened into the onions and there is no watery liquid left. Stir in the Gorgonzola, if using. Season with salt and plenty of pepper. Leave to cool.

Next, the pastry. Put all the ingredients into a bowl and mix together to form a smooth, glossy dough. Divide in half and roll each half into a ball. If the filling isn't cool yet, cover the pastry with clingfilm and stash in the fridge.

Preheat the oven to 200°C/180°C fan/gas 6. Roll the first ball of pastry out to form a large, thin circle. Don't worry about perfection. Lay on a baking tray lined with baking parchment. Spread the filling over the pastry, leaving a 2cm bare border. Roll the remaining pastry out to make a circle of about the same size. Lay this over the filling, then fold the edges over to seal, neatening up the rough bits as you go.

Prick the surface all over with a fork, make a hole in the centre for steam to escape, then brush lightly with beaten egg. Bake for 30 minutes, until richly browned.

Serve hot, warm or cold.

One *puccia*, two *pucce*, many *puccerie*

Attaching the suffix *'eria'* to a foodstuff is the neatest way to denote a shop or café or restaurant specialising in said foodstuff. So, within a few minutes' walk from my house there is a *kebabberia*, many *pizzerie*, a *pescheria* (fishmonger's), a *tabaccheria* (okay, so it applies to non-foodstuffs as well) and a *birreria* (and to drinks). Disappointingly there actually isn't a *pucceria*, although I can buy vacuum-packed *pucce* from Mimmo's Salumeria (salami and cured meats) just around the corner.

Puccerie sell filled *pucce*. And a *puccia* is a thick, flat bread disc that is warmed through, halved and filled. Essentially we're talking about the Puglian equivalent of the sandwich shop. Some are pretty basic, others are just fabulous. I have a particular fondness for the tiny hectic Pucciaria in Santo Spirito, a suburb of Bari, and the Baguetteria de Pace in Gallipoli, but no doubt I will be adding plenty more to the list as I find them.

Wikipedia claims that pizza chef (and carpenter, well why not?), Giovanni Caccetta, initiated the *puccia* craze from his small restaurant in the town of Trepuzzi, some time in the 1970s, inspired by the way housewives used up the last scraps of pizza dough. He recognised a good thing and saw that this 'crumbless' flattish bread would be just the ticket for a quick snack. Crumbless, by the way, in the sense that there is precious little soft centre compared to the chewy exterior. Later, his daughter and her husband grabbed the baton and opened the first dedicated *pucceria* in Brindisi. I've got a feeling, though, that its roots go way back into the past. No coincidence, surely, that they have emerged from what was once Magna Graecia. Town names like Calimera, Gallipoli and Monopoli are lingering ghosts of long extinguished Hellenic communities, and the Griko dialect is still spoken in a few towns in the south.

Much changes over two or three thousand years, but really *pucce* are just thicker, rounder pitta breads. Like pitta they come with a hollow centre – not quite so pronounced but there all the same.

Most of the recipes I've seen for *pucce* combine different flours in varying proportions. I love the taste and colour of semolina flour (see page 121), softened with plain flour, but strong white bread flour works well, too. The important thing is to make the dough loose enough to shape easily. In other words, work a good amount of water into the flour to produce a sticky soft mass. If kneading is hard work, then your dough is not sufficiently hydrated. Knead in more water, little by little, until the dough is blissfully smooth and relaxed and plumptious. Semolina flour, by the way, will absorb more water than white bread flour.

Pucce

'Crumbless' Flattish Sandwich Breads

Makes 6

400g semolina flour or strong white bread flour, plus a little extra for the baking trays
100g plain flour
2 teaspoons salt
1 x 7g sachet of fast-action dried yeast or 15g fresh yeast
4 tablespoons extra virgin olive oil, plus a little extra for oiling the bowl
300–400ml warm water

Mix the flours and salt in a bowl. If using dried yeast, mix that in as well. If using fresh yeast, make a well in the centre, fill with a good slurp of the warm water, then crumble the yeast into it. Work the yeast into the water with your fingers. Add the olive oil, then mix into the flour along with enough water to form a soft, slightly sticky dough.

Knead on a lightly floured work surface for 10 minutes or so, until smooth, elastic and gorgeously cushiony. Roll into a ball. Drizzle a little oil into the mixing bowl, turn the dough in it so that it is nicely oiled, then cover with a beeswax cloth or clingfilm. Leave to rise in a warm place until doubled in volume.

Preheat the oven to 250°C/230°C fan/gas 9. Line 2 baking trays with baking parchment and sprinkle with semolina flour or strong white bread flour. Divide the dough into 6. Roll each piece into a ball. Cover lightly and leave for 15 minutes.

One at a time, transfer the balls to the lined baking trays and, using your fingers, press and dimple them into discs no more than 1cm thick. Again, cover lightly and set aside for 10 minutes. Bake for 15 minutes, or until lightly browned and puffed. Cool on a wire rack.

Fillings for *pucce*

For the full *puccia* experience, begin by warming your *puccia* through in the toaster or under the grill. Then split in half horizontally, drizzle a little olive oil over the cut sides and pile in the fillings.

Obviously, you can fill them with whatever you like, but if you want to echo the Puglian experience, here are a few suggestions:

Marinated and grilled octopus (see page 105) and tomato

Prosciutto crudo, mozzarella and tomato

Cotto (cooked ham), mozzarella and rocket

Chicken, garlic mayonnaise and radicchio

Mortadella, *scamorza* cheese and grilled peppers

Soft pecorino, radicchio and tomato

Pizzi Leccesi

Craggy Tomato and Olive Rolls

Modern *pucce* are, as far as I can tell, derivatives of *pizzi leccesi* or *mpilli* or *puccette* depending on where they are made. These are craggy little rolls that would once have been made with the last of a large batch of bread dough and whatever else was to hand in the kitchen. An end-of-the-line treat, best eaten still warm from the oven, though they keep well enough in an airtight container for a couple of days. There are endless variations not only on the name but also on the 'seasoning' ingredients. In some versions it is just a question of adding handfuls of olives or pancetta cubes, in others there are raw cubes of courgette, or onion or tomato.

This recipe with the addition of cooked tomato, onion and olives is particularly irresistible. I avoid skinning tomatoes on the whole, but here it makes a noticeable difference, encouraging the tomatoes to melt down to a thick sauce. Once you mix the tomatoey goo into the *pucce* dough, you will end up with an absurdly sticky mixture. This is not a mistake. Go with the flow, think childish mud-pie squelchy thoughts, and all will be well.

Makes 12–14

1 quantity of *pucce* dough (see page 135)
1 onion, sliced
1 medium-hot red chilli, fresh or dried, finely chopped
2 tablespoons extra virgin olive oil
400g tomatoes, skinned and roughly chopped
1 tablespoon tomato purée
100g black olives, stoned

salt
extra flour (semolina flour or strong white bread flour), for shaping

Make the *pucce* dough, then cover and leave to rise until doubled in volume. This should take around an hour, depending on the warmth of the room.

Meanwhile make the filling. Fry the onion and the chilli, if using a fresh one, very gently in the olive oil until the onion is very soft and golden. Now add the dried chilli, if using, and cook for a minute or so longer. Add the tomatoes and the tomato purée to the pan. Give it all a good stir, then leave to cook gently, stirring and squidging the tomato pieces every now and then. Scrape the bottom of the pan if it threatens to catch. After 15–20 minutes or so, the tomatoes should have softened down to a thick pulp. If it is still a bit on the watery side, leave it to cook for a few minutes longer. Stir in the olives and turn off the heat. Taste and add salt if it needs it. Leave to cool.

Put 4 or 5 heaped tablespoons of flour into a bowl and line a baking tray with baking parchment. Preheat the oven to 220°C/200°C fan/gas 7.

Knock back the bread dough. Add the tomato and olive mixture. Now the messiness begins: squelch it into the dough with your hands. Keep going. At first it feels like it will never meld in, but after a few more minutes of anxious manipulation it really will come together as one very wet and sticky mass. Scrape the dough off your fingers as well as you can but don't bother washing them yet. There's really no point. Sprinkle a little of the flour on to your hands and then scoop out a heaped palmful of the dough. Shape it roughly into a ball, then turn it in the bowl of flour and place on the lined baking tray. Repeat until you've used up all the dough. You should end up with 12–14 knobbly heaps of dough.

Cover loosely with a beeswax cloth or a plastic bag and set aside for 10 minutes in a warm place. Uncover and slide into the oven. Bake for 15–20 minutes, until the underneath of each roll is nicely browned and sounds hollow when tapped. Leave to cool on a wire rack.

Nothing is original

Whatever anyone claims, 99.99% of chefs and cooks do not create original recipes. We all build on what others have done before us, tweaking, replacing one ingredient with something newish (at least to our own regional pantries) or unexpected, borrowing from elsewhere, hopefully improving, often diminishing dishes that have stood the test of time for good reason, refining, deconstructing or prettifying. Assertions of originality imply lack of knowledge or laziness on the part of reviewers or reporters or caterers themselves. The Ferran Adriás of this world are rarer than Burmese painite (look it up).

In my almost four decades of churning out recipes, I have grown to loathe the editor's request for blah blah 'with a twist'. Still, a few months ago I came up with a genius twist on a classic, one that made use of a plentiful local Pugliese ingredient that is usually poured down the drain. Hah! Reducing food waste as well! A light-bulb moment indeed.

When I proudly told my son that mozzarella water was a brilliant substitute for buttermilk when making soda bread (which it is), he nodded. 'Yup, that's exactly what the café/bakery I used to work for used leftover mozzarella whey for.' Personal originality balloon instantly burst. Nothing is original in the kitchen.

While I'm at it, I'd also like to thank my friend Wendy, who put me on to the idea of using up leftover Christmas mincemeat in a batch of soda bread, and old chums Darina and Timmy Allen, who first introduced me to Irish Spotty Dog, raisin-heavy soda bread. Here then, is my very unoriginal but tasty Italian version.

Cane Macchiato

Italian Spotted Dog

Makes 1 loaf – plenty for 8 people

450g 00 pasta flour
1 level teaspoon salt
1 level tablespoon bicarbonate of soda or baking powder
175g Italianish orange and walnut mincemeat (see page 267), or the leftover Christmas mincemeat at the back of your fridge
1 egg
50ml mozzarella water or buttermilk
caster or granulated sugar

Preheat the oven to 220°C/200°C fan/gas 7. Line a baking tray with baking parchment.

Mix the flour with the salt and bicarbonate of soda or baking powder. Make a well in the centre and add the mincemeat, the egg and the mozzarella water or buttermilk. Mix to a soft dough. Shape into a nice round loaf and settle it on the lined baking tray. Dredge the loaf with a generous coat of caster or granulated sugar, then, with your sharpest knife, slash a cross across the surface.

Bake for 20 minutes, then reduce the oven temperature to 190°C/170°C fan/gas 5 and bake for a further 30–40 minutes. It's done when it sounds hollow when tapped on the bottom. Let it cool for a couple of minutes, then transfer to a wire rack to cool at least until it can be eaten without burning.

Serve warm, with lots of salted butter.

5

THE ELIXIR OF LIFE

Driving out of Bari airport, in just a few miles you enter Puglia's most characteristic landscape, the endless olive groves stretching away on either side. It's a warm welcome to the new arrival, a promise of good food around the corner, the first glimpse of the region's life force. For locals it's a sign of homecoming and reassurance. There's a sense of continuity and connection. However much the world changes, however much technology advances, the olive tree and the olive harvest and, above all, the olive oil remain true and strong and eternal.

Of course, you could say much the same of any number of regions around the Mediterranean, but Puglians value their olive trees so much that they put one right in the centre of their coat of arms. There it stands, strong and sure, a symbol of peace and brotherhood, surrounded by a blue octagon that represents the magnificent Castel del Monte, and above it the crown of Frederick the Second, Holy Roman Emperor, *stupor mundi, puer Apuliae* (wonder of the world, son of Apulia), emblazoned with six gold coins, or bezants if you want to be technical, one for each of Puglia's six provinces.

Here's a strange thing – for all that olive trees are ten a penny and common as muck, for all that every family seems to own their own little *uliveto,* their olive grove with enough trees to produce olive oil to last throughout the year, for all that the silver-green leaves are more plentiful than grass, for all of that, olive trees still retain an air of majesty and grandeur and ancient wisdom. They are special, silent witnesses to human life and folly.

It's not uncommon to find trees that have been providing fruit for hundreds of years. There is an official Register of Monumental Olive Trees which includes many *ultramillenari* trees that date back not just centuries but two or three millennia, each one numbered and listed and treasured. They are amazing beings, with their enormous, twisted, gnarled trunks. It is a strange feeling indeed to stand in their shade, in the very same place where 2,000 years ago some Roman peasant stood to escape the heat, and before her a Messapian (from the tribe that bequeathed its name to my town, Ceglie Messapica), way back before Christ, or Muhammad or even Buddha, was a twinkle in anyone's eye.

For a long time Puglia has been Italy's biggest olive oil producer, but not for much longer. The mighty reign of the olive tree is under attack, and the olive is losing. A tragedy is unfolding. As you drive southwards, past Brindisi, towards Lecce, the destruction is all around you. For kilometres and kilometres the road passes through fields of dead olive trees, gaunt leafless ghosts in a post-apocalyptic landscape. It is devastating.

Nobody seems to be able to prevent the relentless march of the demon *Xyllella fastidiosa.* This malign bacteria tip-toed into Puglia some time between 2008 and 2010, quietly making itself at home in olive groves around the town of Gallipoli, which is where I caught my first glimpse of the havoc it wreaks. It had hitched a ride, so the story goes, on a cargo of ornamental plants from Costa Rica.

It was first identified in 2013. In seven short years it has spread like wildfire, carried by spittlebugs from *uliveto* to *uliveto,* sucking olive trees dry and dead. Now you can see it settling in slyly through the Itria Valley. Friends of mine have the tell-tale signs in their patches of land. It starts with one brown, desiccated branch among the lush silver-green foliage. A few olive varieties are more resistant than the rest, but those extraordinary *ultramillenari* trees are not immune.

There is some small hope on the horizon. A new organic treatment that boosts the immune system of the olive trees is looking promising, but it may be too little too late. The thought of a Puglia bereft of olive trees is too grim to contemplate, but that's the way it could go if those with the money and the power don't put more of both into supporting research and olive farmers across the region. This is the Covid-19 of the olive trees, destroying not only the trees themselves but also the livelihoods of thousands of people involved in production as well as a cherished way of life.

A fine weekend for picking

Mother Nature is on my side. Early November and the sun is shining fit to burst. The olives are ripening nicely and beginning to drop from the trees. For the next few days I'm a vagabond for hire, my fee a litre or two of fresh olive oil. Inevitably I oversleep and by the time I arrive at my first destination the green nets are spread out around the trees and one pink plastic crate is already full of taut-skinned olives.

This is my first olive harvest ever and I set to with all the enthusiasm of a novice. Yellow plastic rake in hand, I comb out olives, determined to pull every last one from the lower branches. On one side Dave is thwacking the upper branches with a long sturdy stick, pelting olives down around me. 'Wear old clothes,' he cautioned a few days earlier, and it's not long before my top is splotched with purplish, oily stains. He confides that he even has a special pair of olive-picking pants that only emerge from the back of the cupboard for these few days of the year.

Two days later, we reconvene at the *frantoio*, the oil mill, just as the sun is setting. We wait our turn in the warm evening glow, watching the silhouettes of new arrivals as they unload their hauls of olives. All around us are walls of ginormous crates, stacked up two storeys high, each one weighed, labelled and in the long queue for the mechanical crushers and squeezers and filterers that are set to transform the raw fruit into limpid green-gold oil. It's a process that is as old as the gods and the output is as valued now as it has been for millennia.

Ancient *frantoi ipogei*, underground oil presses, dotted throughout Puglia, bear witness to this. In Gallipoli alone there were some thirty-five underground presses, some of which can still be visited. Deep under the city, in caves lit only by lanterns and candles, the heavy stone milling-wheels were turned by horses who lived their entire working lives underground. These must have been hellish places to work, reeking of sweat and horseshit, hot and airless, with rats scuttling across dark corners. For the most part, they produced low-grade *lampante* oil, literally oil for lamps and lighting.

In contrast the grand *masserie*, semi-fortified farmhouses, often had their own above-ground olive presses, again with massively heavy stone grinding-wheels dragged round and round by horses or donkeys. Many *masserie* have been transformed into boutique hotels or homes for the rich, with the crushing basins cleaned up, repaired and magicked into fountains, flowerbeds or sculptural elements in elegant, whitewashed courtyards. Others are less cherished. Exploring an abandoned *masseria* near the town of Oria, we wandered into a vast, vaulted hall that ran down the length of the main courtyard. Beams of sunlight lit up the old oil press in the centre, littered with empty beer cans and debris. Red graffiti on the opposite wall read: *'Maria Grazia, la Mia Vita!!!'*

Olive Dolci Fritti al Pomodoro

Fried Sweet Olives with Tomato

The season for these strangest of olives is early, a few weeks only in September through to October. To the uninitiated, the trees are indistinguishable until the skin of sweet olives darkens to a blue-purple inkiness, in stark contrast to the neighbouring olives, still green and hard on the majority of trees. Crates of sweet olives in the greengrocery look like a harvest of British sloes, but the taste bears no resemblance other than that neither are particularly pleasant to eat raw.

These olives are not necessarily pressed for oil, though they may be salted and preserved in much the same way as the main crop of olives. Mostly, though, they are fried in hot olive oil, with a little salt, until the interior softens. The result is one of the strangest things I have tasted in many years. The sweetness is evident, but these fried olives are uniquely aromatic, bitter, tender and eventually addictive. An acquired taste, to be sure, but their very oddity steals up on you seductively.

Serves 4–6

250g ripe *olive dolci* (sweet olives)
extra virgin olive oil
2 cloves of garlic, thinly sliced
100g cherry tomatoes, quartered
coarse salt

Wash the olives, discard any stems and debris, then let them dry thoroughly.

Cover the base of a frying pan with a decent layer of olive oil – we're talking 0.25cm or so. Heat over a high flame until exceptionally hot. Roll the olives into the pan. Fry for a few minutes, until the flesh between skin and stone is meltingly soft. Add the garlic, stir, then cook for a minute or so more until beginning to colour. Tip in the tomatoes and season with salt. Stir for just a few more seconds, so that the tomato is as hot as the olives, but not yet collapsing into sauce, then scoop it all out on to a plate. Eat as soon as you can without burning your mouth, with a thick slice of bread to soak up juices and oil.

Olive Dolci Fritte ai Peperoni

Fried Sweet Olives with Red Peppers

As above, but delete the tomatoes. Instead, deseed and cut half a small red pepper into thin strips. Fry them for a few minutes in the olive oil all on their own, to give them a head start. Now add the sweet olives and fry as above. When they are virtually done, toss in the chopped garlic and fry for a minute or so longer. Scoop out and eat *subito*, again with a thick slice of good bread.

The Sott'Olios

Let me introduce you to the Sott'Olio family, big players in Puglian culture, though they have branches right across Italy. No relation, by the way, to the Dell'Olios, whose striking daughter, Nancy, once dated the Swedish manager of the England national football team, and who genuinely are from Bisceglie in Puglia.

The Sott'Olios are a remarkable clan, colourful, vibrant, often piquant, who mix well with others and can bring any party to life. The name literally means 'under oil' and this family of preserves is a big player on the Italian table.

In a land where olive oil is plentiful it comes as no surprise that it is used to preserve practically anything savoury and edible. The elderly owner of a café in Ostuni told me all about the *tordi*, thrushes that were once a regular treat in the town until hunters all but wiped them out. They shot so many that they had to be preserved for winter, either in olive oil or in white wine. He went quite misty-eyed with pleasurable remembrance.

These days, thankfully, vegetables predominate on the *sott'olio* scene. The method is, for the most part, pretty similar whatever is being *sott'olio*-ed. The vegetable is cleaned and suitably peeled, sliced or diced. Those with a high water content may be salted overnight, then squeezed dry. Others will be blanched for a few minutes in watered-down vinegar and herbs or spices. Some are chargrilled to soften them just the right amount. And then it's simple, submerge them in olive oil and store in a dark cupboard for the months when said veg is no longer in season.

My favourite *sott'olio* is definitely downstairs Maria's *pipone*, made with red peppers and chilli. My son prefers her aubergine *sott'olio*. Here are the recipes for both.

Melanzane Sott'Olio

Aubergine Pickles

Makes 3–4 x 330ml jars

2kg firm glossy aubergines
140g salt
500ml white wine vinegar
6 red chillies, thinly sliced
6 cloves of garlic, sliced
500–700ml extra virgin olive oil
16–20 mint leaves

Peel the aubergines, then cut them into 1cm-thick slices. Sprinkle about half the salt on trays, lay the aubergine slices on top in a single layer, then sprinkle with the remaining salt. Cover loosely and ignore them for 3 hours. Tip them into a large colander and let all the salty liquid drain away. Rinse and dry the trays, then line them with clean tea towels.

Cut the salted aubergine into 0.5cm-wide strips. Put the vinegar and 500ml of water into a saucepan and bring to the boil. Tip in the aubergine strips together with the chillies and garlic. Bring back to the boil, then simmer for 30 seconds and no more. Drain quickly. As soon as they are cool enough to handle, gather up handfuls of strips (with the garlic and chilli) and squeeze hard to eliminate as much moisture as possible. Spread them out on the tea towels and leave for an hour or so. Replace the tea towels with new dry ones and leave for another hour or two, until the strips are dry to the touch.

Meanwhile sterilise your jam jars (see note on page 246). Pour a thin layer of olive oil into the bottom of the first one, then pack in a layer of aubergine/chilli/garlic and add a couple of leaves of mint. Pour in enough oil to almost cover. Repeat until the jar is full, leaving a 1cm or so gap at the top. It's important to make sure that the final layer of oil completely covers the aubergines. Tap the jars gently on the work surface to expel lingering air bubbles, add a little more oil if needed, then seal tightly. Fill the remaining jars in the same way. Either store in the fridge where they will keep nicely for 2–3 months, or water-process them (see page 156) for longer storage in a cool, dark cupboard. Either way, hold back for at least 2 weeks before digging in.

Pipone

Red Pepper Olive Oil Pickles
(cooked in a domestic oven)

Downstairs Maria actually makes two different versions of *pipone*. For the first, the peppers are not cooked at all, just salted and squeezed dry before ladling into jars and topping up with olive oil. If you are short on time this works well and the results are good. Better still, however, is the *pipone* with peppers cooked gently in the oil in her wood-fired oven. Just divine! This recipe hovers somewhere between the two and is the one I make for myself and people I really, really like.

Makes 2–3 x 330ml jars

around 750g red peppers
2–4 red chillies
1 chunky stem of celery
20g salt
200ml extra virgin olive oil
2 cloves of garlic, chopped

Day 1

Quarter the red peppers, then remove the seeds and stalks and the white membrane. Dice into little pieces around 1cm square. Snip or chop the red chillies into small rings. Remove the seeds if you want to. Cut the celery in half lengthways, then slice thinly. Mix these three in a bowl with the salt. Tip into a colander, set over a bowl. Find a plate that will fit inside the colander, not too tightly, slide it in, then put a heavy weight on top. I used my cast iron mortar, but tins of tomatoes or whatever you have to hand will do just fine. Transfer the peppers to the fridge and leave to drain for 12 hours or overnight, mixing them up once or twice during that time, so that they are evenly pressed.

Day 2

Preheat the oven to 140°C/120°C fan/gas 1. Use your hands to squeeze out the last drops of moisture from the peppers, then tip them into a roasting tin or wide, ovenproof casserole dish. Add the oil and the garlic. Stir, then cover with foil and slide into the oven. Cook gently for 2 hours, stirring every half hour or so.

Now discard the foil, stir again and slide back into the oven. Cook for another half an hour. By now the peppers will have shrunk and lost virtually all their residual moisture, darkening to a deep brick red. Cool slightly.

Ladle into hot, sterilised jam jars (see note on page 246), leaving a good 1cm gap at the top. Seal tightly. Either store in the fridge, or water-process them for long-term storage (see page 156, it's not half as complicated as you might imagine).

Raw Pepper Pipone

If you want to try out the raw pepper version, salt and drain the peppers as above. Squeeze out all the remaining moisture with your hands. Pour a little olive oil into your jam jars, add a decent layer of squeezed-out pepper mixture, and pour in enough olive oil to cover. Repeat until the jars are full and the peppers are all used up. Make sure that they are completely covered in oil. If you go down this route you absolutely must water-process them before storage (see below). Once processed, label and leave for at least a week before sampling.

How to water-process pickles for long storage

For this you will need a huge saucepan with a lid, several clean tea towels and large kitchen tongs. Begin by scrumpling a couple of tea towels over the bottom of the pan. Arrange your filled, sealed jars upright in the pan, with more tea towels curled between them to prevent them bumping into each other. Pour in enough water to cover the jars. Bring to the boil, then boil for 20–30 minutes. Carefully lift the jars out with the tongs and let them dry. Label and hide them in a cool, dark cupboard.

Chocolate Olive Oil Mousse

Incredibly rich and incredibly gorgeous. That's probably all I need say, except that even the locals think it sounds weird. Thankfully all misapprehension dissolves once tasted.

Serves 4

100g dark chocolate, finely chopped
2 egg yolks
80g light muscovado sugar
a pinch of salt
4 tablespoons extra virgin olive oil
3 egg whites

To serve
a little extra virgin olive oil
sea salt flakes

Melt the chocolate, then leave to cool for 5 minutes or so. Whisk the egg yolks with the muscovado sugar and a pinch of salt, until the sugar has dissolved. Whisk in the olive oil a little at a time to create a gorgeous voluptuous thick gloop. Whisk the melted chocolate, a slurp or two at a time, into the gloop. You should end up with an even more voluptuous, thick, glossy, chocolaty gloop, but don't panic if it shows ominous signs of graining. Just carry on and all will be fine.

Whisk the egg whites in a separate bowl until they form soft peaks. Fold into the chocolate mixture. Divide between four small bowls or espresso cups or ramekins and chill for a few hours.

Just before serving, drip a few drops of fresh extra virgin olive oil over each mousse, and sprinkle with a few flakes of sea salt.

6

THE STUFF OF LIFE

'La cucina povera' and 'the Mediterranean diet' are terms that are bandied about willy-nilly when we write about Italian food. Between the two of them, they've developed a romantic comfort blanket that wraps warmly around the simpler dishes that make Italian cooking so attractive. 'Aye, we wuz poor but we wuz happy' is the subtext. Merry peasants making the most of the little God gave them, etc. etc. The truth is not so romantic.

For centuries the majority of Italians ate an appallingly sparse and limited diet, particularly in the south. For all but the better-heeled, luxuries such as meat, eggs, dairy products, sugar and coffee were way beyond meagre budgets. Bread or corn (polenta was eaten throughout the length of Italy) was the mainstay, along with legumes, basic vegetables, a little pork fat if they were lucky. Pasta was eaten in select areas but was not a country-wide essential. A couple of slices of hefty bread, made perhaps with chestnut flour or bean flour, and a *companatico*, something to perk up the blandness, an onion for instance or a smear of that pork fat, was a common meal for agricultural workers.

From the Risorgimento, the unification of Italy, in 1861 onwards, successive governments made half-hearted attempts to improve the culinary lot of the average Giuseppe, but it wasn't until after the end of the Second World War that what we now think of as 'the Mediterranean diet' really took root. At last, comparative prosperity meant that most Italians gained access to many of the good things that we associate with Italian cooking: cheeses, cured hams and salamis, fresh meat, focaccia, coffee and *gelato*.

Puglia, like many other regions, was not pasta country, at least not until the second half of the nineteenth century, when bright, shiny new Italy decreed that every able young man should serve five years in the shiny new Italian army. This was where the sons of Puglia learnt to enjoy big plates of *pasta pomodoro* served up on a regular basis. Duty over and done with, they returned home and took their pasta habit with them. Thus Puglia, and all of Italy, became a land of pasta addicts.

In early June the plains of the Tavoliere delle Puglie in the north of Puglia are a carpet of gold stretching out way into the distance. Ripe heads of wheat ripple in the breezes, while above them forests of wind turbines swish round and round as they reap the air above. This is where most of Puglia's durum wheat is grown. High-protein durum wheat is what the best pasta, and the best local bread for that matter, is made with.

You need go only a few paces into Bari's old town before you stumble across canny pasta queens who sit outside their houses making Puglia's favourite pasta, *orecchiette*, little ears. They've learned to monetise a skill they take for granted, smiling for cameras, chatting with their mates, all the while transforming the dough, made of nothing but durum wheat flour and water, into swathes of neat concave discs, ready to dry and sell. Making *orecchiette* is not as simple as they make it look. I've tried and tried, with guidance from expert *orecchiette* makers, and after many substandard attempts I think I may possibly perhaps have cracked the how. It would still take me many hours to make enough to feed a table of hungry Italians.

Like the *orecchiette*, other favoured Puglian pasta shapes such as *cavatelli* (closely related to *orecchiette* but far easier to roll), *strascinati* (a flattened form of *orecchiette*, rough one side, smooth on the other), *minchiareddi* (a form of *maccheroni*), *foglie di ulivo* (oval and green, like olive leaves) and *sagne* (ringlets) are made from the simplest of doughs – just durum wheat, in the form of semolina flour (see page 121) and water – once again a legacy of extreme poverty, when eggs were too valuable to use in a basic dough.

The only pasta shape I've actually mastered is the *minchiareddi* or *maccheroncini*. A small knob of dough, rolled around a metal spoke, called a *ferro*. In a rush of enthusiasm after this small success, I bought eight *ferri* from the market, bundled them into my backpack and set off to the UK to teach a pasta class. Of course, the airport officials at the luggage X-ray machines picked up on them. When I explained that they were for teaching the British how to make Puglian pasta, they cheered and waved me and my *ferri* on through. How I love the Italians!

Grano Arso (Burnt Grain, not Big Arse)

Grano arso is a speciality of the more northerly parts of Puglia, around the Tavoliere, the great wheatfields of Puglia. Before grinding, the dried wheat berries are roasted, just like coffee beans, in large drums until they turn a rich dark brown. The resultant flour is a slatey, purplish pale brown. It's mostly used to make pasta, bringing its mild nutty flavour with it. I like it in biscuits and cakes but that's not strictly Puglian.

This torrefaction process is the modern commercial take on a practice that goes back to a less calculated past. After the harvest, the stubble was burnt off to clear the land. The poorest mothers and children then scoured the blackened fields, gathering up any burnt grains they could find among the ashes.

Dirty work for little return, I imagine, but a free meal is a free meal. These days you can buy *grano arso* flour anywhere, but you pay for the privilege.

Two fundamental ways to make your pasta taste even better

1. Put lots of salt into the cooking water. Italian friends insist that it should be as salty as the sea. As you spoon it in, reassure yourself that most of it will remain in the water. 10g of salt, that's 2 teaspoons, per litre of water. Ideally you should also be heating 1 litre of water for each 100g of pasta.
2. Just before draining, scoop out a cupful of the pasta cooking water from the pan. Add a slurp or two as you toss the cooked pasta into its sauce. It will relax the sauce just enough to coat the pasta smoothly, adding a subtle silkiness to the dish from the starch. It's one of the best tricks I know.

Orecchiette alle Cime di Rapa

Orecchiette with Bitter Greens

One of the truly great pasta dishes, for its taste and simplicity and economy. If ever there was something that amounted to more than the sum of its parts, this is surely it. It has become one of my top go-to dishes on a chilly day. You need to start with a minor mountain of greens. Pasta and greens are cooked together for maximum taste, then seasoned with brisk chilli, garlic and anchovy oil. The partial collapse of the greens is an essential component of the dish, so don't fuss about over-cooking.

Cime di rapa (usually translated as turnip greens but not quite the same as the green leaves that come out of the top of a turnip) are a rarity outside of Italy, but purple sprouting broccoli is a decent stand-in. American collard greens are similar.

Orecchiette alle cime di rapa is sometimes served with 'poor man's Parmesan', in other words, crisp, golden fried breadcrumbs, but grated cheese is considered a no-no. Still, in the privacy of my kitchen, I break the rule with a sprinkle of freshly grated pecorino or Parmesan. Try it without first, to taste it as it should be, then add as you will.

Serves 4

salt
600–800g *cime di rapa*, or purple sprouting broccoli
400g fresh *orecchiette*, or 350g dried *orecchiette*
6 tablespoons extra virgin olive oil

3 cloves of garlic, thinly sliced
1–2 fresh or dried red chillies, roughly chopped, seeds and all
3 or 4 anchovies, chopped

Fresh *orecchiette*

Put a large, well-salted pot of water on to boil. Rinse the *cime di rapa* thoroughly to get rid of inevitable grit (especially after heavy rainfall). Trim off the tougher, thickest stalks and discard. Slash the leaves and stems roughly into pieces 3 or 4cm long. Precision is not required. Toss them all into the boiling water, give them a stir, then simmer for around 5 minutes. Add the *orecchiette*, stir again, and cook for a final 2–3 minutes, until the pasta is al dente.

As soon as the *orecchiette* are in the pan, put the oil, garlic, chillies and anchovies into a frying pan. Heat up and fry until the garlic is hinting at brown. Do not let the garlic burn. By now the pasta and greens will be cooked. Scoop out a cupful or ladleful of the pasta water and reserve. Drain swiftly, then tip into the frying pan. Toss with the oil, garlic, chillies and anchovies and a slurp or two of the reserved pasta water until all are mixed and hot. Eat at once.

Dried *orecchiette*

The method is pretty much the same as above, except for timings. So, once your water is boiling, add the orecchiette and the *cime di rapa* together. Start heating the oil, garlic, chillies and anchovies a couple of minutes before the orecchiette and greens are ready, and finish as for fresh *orecchiette*.

Cavatelli con Polpette di Pane, Melanzane e Sugo

Cavatelli Pasta with Bread Fritters and Aubergine in Tomato Sauce

Puglian cooks are well-versed in making a feast out of very little. Bread fritters in tomato sauce on pasta sounds uninspiring, but don't be fooled – it's a terrific combination. My neighbour, Maria, serves it in the classic Italian two-course style. In other words, pasta and sauce first, followed by warm tomato-soaked fritters. I'm more of an all-in-one sort of a person. Either way it is an excellent filling meat-free main course, great for vegetarians as long as you use a vegetarian alternative to pecorino or Parmesan.

The thing here is to make a big batch of bread fritters (see page 198) for friends or family, but to hide away around half of them (cool, cover and stash in the fridge, or freeze until needed), to make your *cavatelli con polpette di pane* the next day.

Serves 4

1 medium-large aubergine, trimmed and cut into 1–2cm dice
extra virgin olive oil
1 onion, chopped
3 cloves of garlic, finely chopped
3 tablespoons roughly chopped flat-leaf parsley
500ml passata
1 heaped teaspoon dried oregano
salt and freshly ground black pepper
a pinch or two of sugar, if required

350g dried *cavatelli*, or 400g fresh
½ quantity of cooked *polpette di pane* (see page 198)
1 heaped tablespoon capers, rinsed if salted
freshly grated pecorino, Parmesan or Grano Padano

If you have time, put the aubergine cubes into a colander, sprinkle with salt, toss to mix, then leave to drain for 30–60 minutes. This isn't essential, but they will absorb a little less oil as they fry.

For the sauce, put 4 tablespoons of olive oil, the chopped onion, garlic and parsley into a pan. Place over a moderate heat. Heat to a lazy sizzle, then reduce the heat a little and leave to cook gently for a good 10 minutes, without browning, stirring occasionally, until the onion is meltingly tender and translucent. Tip in the passata, oregano, salt and pepper, and a small glass of water. Bring to the boil, then reduce the heat again and simmer for 10 minutes or so. Stir occasionally, and add a little more water if it gets too thick and spitty. Taste and adjust the seasoning, adding a pinch or two of sugar if it is on the sharp side.

Put a pan of water on to boil, adding plenty of salt. Cook the *cavatelli* according to the packet instructions. Before draining, scoop out and reserve a mugful or ladleful of the cooking water.

Meanwhile, heat another 3 tablespoons of olive oil in a wide frying pan. Heat well, then add half the aubergine cubes. Sauté until golden brown more or less all over. Scoop out on to a plate lined with kitchen paper, then add the rest of the aubergine to the pan, with another slurp of olive oil, and repeat. Drain with the rest of the aubergine.

Pile the aubergine, *polpette di pane* and capers into the tomato sauce. Cook for a few minutes to heat the whole shebang through thoroughly. Taste and adjust the seasoning. Tip the cooked pasta into the sauce (or vice versa if that's easier). Mix well, adding a little of the reserved pasta water if the sauce is too claggy. Serve with freshly grated pecorino.

Pasta al Forno di Ferragosto

Pasta Gratin with Meatballs

Ferragosto, the 15th of August, is a big family holiday right across Italy. Kind of like Christmas or Thanksgiving but very hot and without the presents. It's a clan thing; grandparents, sons and daughters, grandchildren, aunts, uncles, cousins and any strays they care to round up all gather in the searing summer heat, to enjoy a ginormous meal around a ginormous table (or more likely several tables jammed together).

In my first summer here, I was honoured to be invited to the Altavista/Urgesi family feast. We gathered at their country patch, amid olive and fig trees, and ate until we could barely move. This is the menu:

Antipasto: Melon and *prosciutto crudo*, mozzarella *nodini* (knots), *polpette di carne*.

Primo: Maria's magnificent *pasta al forno*, complete with meatballs, mozzarella, mortadella and ham, baked in the wood-fired oven.

Secondo: a startling quantity of grilled meats (cooked in the outdoor fireplace), dished up with wedges of lemon and a salad of tomato and real wild rocket picked from the surrounding fields.

Dolci: Peaches, watermelon, *spumoni* (layers of ice cream and liqueur-soaked sponge cake) and my mother's British sweetmeat cake, which is always a winner (see recipe on page 269).

This is my recreation of the undoubted star of the whole meal, Maria's *pasta al forno.*

Serves 8

400g *maccheroncini* or penne
a generous handful of basil leaves
½ quantity of meatballs (see page 59)
500g mozzarella, cut into small cubes
200g aged *caciocavallo, provolone* or mature Cheddar
100g fresh peas, or frozen peas, defrosted
100g cooked ham, diced or cut into short strips
100g mortadella or good salami, skinned and diced or cut into short strips
100g freshly grated pecorino or Parmesan
extra virgin olive oil, for drizzling

For the sauce
5 tablespoons extra virgin olive oil, plus a little extra for the dish
1 large onion, sliced
6 cloves of garlic, chopped
1.5kg ripe tomatoes, skinned and puréed, or 1.5 litres passata and a big squirt of tomato purée
a generous handful of basil leaves
salt and freshly ground black pepper
a little sugar (optional)
4 tablespoons capers, rinsed if salted

Leave plenty of time for making the tomato sauce and the meatballs. I usually make them both the day before.

For the sauce, put the olive oil and onion into a large pan and cook over a lowish heat, stirring occasionally, until the onion is very tender. Raise the heat a little and add the garlic, fry for another minute or two, then pour in the puréed tomatoes, or passata and tomato purée, together with half a litre of water. Stir in a big handful of basil leaves and season with a little salt and lots of freshly ground black pepper. Simmer gently, partially covered, for at least an hour, better still 2 hours, stirring occasionally and adding more water whenever it gets too thick and threatens to catch on the bottom. The finished sauce should be fairly thick, but still runny. Taste and adjust the seasonings, adding a little sugar if it tastes too tart. Stir in the capers. Leave to cool.

Preheat the oven to 200°C/180°C fan/gas 6. Pour a little olive oil into a large baking dish and smear it around the base and sides. Cook the pasta in plenty of salted boiling water until almost but not quite cooked. Scoop out a mugful of the cooking water and reserve, then drain the pasta.

Mix the pasta, the tomato sauce, another big handful of basil, the meatballs, mozzarella, *caciocavallo*, peas, ham and mortadella together. Add a few slurps of pasta water if it looks a little dry. Tip into the prepared dish and smooth down. Sprinkle thickly with pecorino, and drizzle a thin trickle of olive oil over the top. Bake for 30–40 minutes, until sizzlingly hot and browned. Let it cool for a few minutes, then serve.

Orecchiette al Primitivo di Manduria

Orecchiette with Red Wine and Meatballs

Manduria, south of Taranto, is the centre of the main Primitivo wine-growing area of Puglia. Primitivo is wonderfully lush, deep purple-red nectar. I stayed here for four days when I first arrived in Puglia, amid torrential rain. This dish, and a big glass of Primitivo to wash it down, put the damp world around me to rights.

If you are in a tearing hurry, you can replace the meatballs with good sausages, cut into chunks before frying, but don't cut costs with a cheap wine substitute.

Serves 4

1 quantity of meatball mixture (see page 59)
extra virgin olive oil

And the rest
1 red onion, chopped
salt
350g *orecchiette*
250ml Primitivo wine

To serve
a little roughly chopped flat-leaf parsley
freshly grated pecorino or Parmesan

Roll the meatball mixture into small balls. Size-wise we're talking around 2–2.5cm in diameter.

Heat 2 tablespoons of olive oil in a wide frying pan over a moderately lively heat. Add the meatballs (you should hear a hissing sizzle as they hit the oil – if you don't, then it isn't hot enough). Fry for a few minutes without disturbing, then shake the pan gently, to roll them over. Fry until browned, scoop out and set aside.

Return the pan to a gentle heat, and add 2 more tablespoons of olive oil and the onion. Cook gently for about 10 minutes until very, very tender.

Meanwhile, bring a large pan of water to the boil, and salt generously. Add the *orecchiette* and simmer until al dente (check packet instructions for timing). Scoop out a cupful of the cooking water and reserve. Drain the pasta.

Reheat the onion if necessary, then pour in the wine and let it sizzle for a minute or two until reduced by about half. Tip in the meatballs and any juice they've given off. Heat through, stirring so that the balls are all dyed a lush dark purple-brown. Now pile in the cooked pasta and add 2 or 3 tablespoons of the reserved pasta water. Stir so that the pasta, too, is stained purple. Add a little more of the reserved pasta water if it seems dry, but remember that it is not a dish that should be swamped in sauce.

Serve hot from the pan, sprinkled with parsley, and with oodles of freshly grated cheese.

Brasciole al Sugo

Slow-cooked Beef or Veal Rolls in Tomato Sauce

Brasciole al sugo is a multipurpose dish, a bit like a warm, wide snuggly scarf that works as comfortingly as a shawl or a throw or muffler. Here are five possible styles for you to try on:

Style 1: Toss pasta into the *brasciole* sauce, and serve with a *brasciola* or two perched on top.

Style 2: Serve most of the sauce on pasta, and make the *brasciole*, kept warm in the remaining sauce, your main course.

Style 3: Serve the *brasciole*, warmed in a little of their sauce, as part of an antipasto, then use the rest of the sauce on pasta for your main course, or a subsequent meal.

Style 4: Serve the *brasciole* hot in plenty of sauce, with soft polenta or mashed potato.

Style 5: Use the sauce to make a simple *pasta al forno* topped with grated cheese and breadcrumbs, and slice cold *brasciole* thickly to slide into panini or sandwiches with rocket and mozzarella. Two distinct meals in one.

Note that you will have to ask your butcher to cut the slices of beef or veal for you; they need to be no more than 0.25cm thick at most.

Serves 4

For the brasciole
8 thin slices of beef or veal flank or skirt steak (total weight around 500g)
salt and freshly ground black pepper
80g pancetta lardons
1 small bunch of flat-leaf parsley, chopped, stems and all
2 cloves of garlic, chopped
3 tablespoons capers, rinsed if salted
8 heaped teaspoons freshly grated pecorino

For the sauce
4 tablespoons extra virgin olive oil
1 onion, chopped
1 carrot, finely diced
1 stem of celery, finely diced
3 cloves of garlic, chopped
150ml white or red wine
1 litre passata

For styles 1, 2 and 3
350g *orecchiette, cavatelli, sagne* or tagliatelle
more freshly grated pecorino

You will need at least 16 wooden cocktail sticks or some kitchen string.

Begin with the *brasciole* themselves. Gently bash each slice of meat to spread it out even more thinly. Lay them all out in front of you. Season with salt and pepper. In the centre of each one pile up the following: 4 cubes of pancetta, roughly ½ tablespoon of parsley, a pinch or two of garlic, about a teaspoon of capers, a heaped teaspoon of pecorino. Reserve the rest of the pancetta and parsley to add to the sauce.

Fold the two opposite sides of the meat over the filling. Fold one of the long flaps over the central mound, then roll right up. Secure each *brasciola* with a couple of wooden cocktail sticks or tie a short length of kitchen string around it.

Now for the sauce. Put the olive oil, onion, carrot, celery, garlic and the remaining pancetta into a decent-sized saucepan or casserole dish with a heavy base. Place over a moderate heat and cook for 5 minutes or so. Nestle the *brasciole* in among the vegetables. Continue frying, turning the *brasciole* every few minutes until they are lightly browned. Pour in the wine and sizzle it away for a minute or so. Next pour in the passata and 500ml of water. Stir in the rest of the parsley and season with salt and pepper. Bring to a simmer, then cover and turn the heat right down low. Leave to simmer quietly for 2 hours. Check it regularly, stirring gently, and adding a few more splashes of water if it threatens to catch on the base. Taste and adjust the seasoning.

Lift the *brasciole* themselves out of the pan, together with a little of the sauce to keep them moist. Keep warm.

Styles 1, 2 and 3: Cook the pasta in a large pan of salted water until al dente. Scoop out a cupful of the cooking water and reserve. Drain the pasta and toss with the *brasciole* sauce, adding a slurp of the reserved pasta water if needed. Scatter over some grated pecorino and serve with, after or before the *brasciole*.

Pasta and Beans

Other cultures might have thrown the dishes of previous poverty out with the bathwater, but not the Italians. Double carb-loaded *minestre* are still loved by home cooks and their families, though they will now be burnished with grated cheese, and may well be followed by a meat dish of some sort. In Rome I've eaten legendary *pasta e ceci*, and here in Puglia I've been sated by the wintery combinations of lentils or chickpeas and pasta in any number of forms. These are the comfort foods of the cold months, satisfying and sustaining, when the *scirocco* or *tramontana* winds howl through the streets dragging damp and cold in their wake.

Pasta e Lenticchie

Pasta and Lentils

Small brown lentils are what you need for this dish, and small pasta to match. So you might opt for *ditalini*, or *cavatelli*, or just use broken-up spaghetti or tagliatelle. Either way what emerges is a dowdy-looking dish of pasta in brown sludge, but it tastes great. A scattering of parsley lifts the mood a little but there's no way this is ever going to win the Instagram lottery. Don't be put off. This is comfort food on a budget and vegan into the bargain, at least until you dredge it with grated cheese.

Serves 4

250g dried brown lentils
5 tablespoons extra virgin olive oil
3 cloves of garlic, chopped
2 red chillies, chopped if fresh, broken into 3 pieces each if dried
1 carrot, diced
1 stem of celery, thinly sliced
1 small onion, sliced
10 cherry tomatoes, halved, or 5 tablespoons passata
500ml (and possibly a little more) water or vegetable stock
a generous handful of flat-leaf parsley, roughly chopped
250g dried short pasta, e.g. fusilli, *conchiglie, ruote* or spaghetti, broken into 5–7cm lengths
salt and freshly ground black pepper

To serve
a little more extra virgin olive oil
a little extra chopped flat-leaf parsley
freshly grated pecorino or Parmesan

Rinse the lentils under the cold tap but don't bother to soak them; there's really no need. Put the olive oil, garlic, chillies, carrot, celery and onion into a roomy saucepan and place over a moderate heat. Cook for 5 minutes or so, until sizzling away nicely. Add the cherry tomatoes, if using, and cook briskly until they begin to collapse. If using passata, add that to the pan and bring up to the boil.

Tip in the lentils, then add the water or stock and the parsley. Simmer until the lentils are tender – about 20 minutes. Now add the pasta, salt and pepper, bring back to the boil and simmer, stirring frequently, until the pasta is just cooked through. By this time the lentils will have started to collapse down and thicken the liquid. Add a splash or two of extra water if it threatens to catch on the base of the pan.

Taste and adjust the seasoning – you're bound to need a little more salt. Serve straight away, drizzling each bowlful with a little fresh olive oil. Sprinkle with parsley and pass around the grated cheese.

Ciceri e Tria

Salento Chickpeas and Pasta

This excellent dish, from the Salento, the southern part of Puglia, is a masterclass in domestic ingenuity. There's the standard *soffritto* of onions, carrot, celery and garlic fried in plentiful olive oil, married with chickpeas and a small amount of tomato, but the clever bit is the pasta itself. Half of it is simmered in the chickpea broth but the rest is fried until crisp and golden brown. It's a nifty combination of textures and flavours, conjured up out of the most basic ingredients.

And it's vegan, until you wallop on the Parmesan or pecorino.

Serves 4

300g dried chickpeas, soaked overnight in cold water
6 tablespoons extra virgin olive oil
1 onion, diced
1 large carrot, diced
1 stem of celery, diced
4 cloves of garlic, chopped
1 big sprig of rosemary
2 red chillies, chopped, with seeds
12 cherry tomatoes, quartered
a big handful of flat-leaf parsley, roughly chopped
salt and freshly ground black pepper

For the pasta
400g 00 pasta flour, plus extra for dusting
1 teaspoon salt
sunflower oil, for deep-frying

To serve
freshly grated pecorino or Parmesan (not strictly necessary, but always a good addition, in my opinion)

Drain the chickpeas and tip them into a saucepan. Cover with fresh cold water and bring up to the boil. Skim off any scum. Simmer until the chickpeas are tender – anything from 30 minutes to 1½ hours, depending on age and size.

Take off the heat and leave to cool in their cooking water. DO NOT DRAIN AND THROW THE WATER DOWN THE SINK.

Next, make the pasta dough. Mix the flour and salt and add enough warm water to make a soft dough. You'll need around 200ml. Knead the dough for around 5–10 minutes, until smooth. Form into a ball, wrap in clingfilm and leave at room temperature for at least 20 minutes.

During this time, put the olive oil, onion, carrot, celery, garlic, rosemary and chillies (with their seeds) into a saucepan large enough to take the chickpeas and pasta as well. This is your *soffritto*, ready to be cooked. Place over a moderate heat and fry the *soffritto* for some 10 minutes or so, until beginning to colour here and there. Tip in the tomatoes and parsley and stir them around in the oil for a minute or two. Next, scoop in all the chickpeas and top with about 1 litre of their cooking water. Season with a little salt. Simmer all this gently together while you finish the pasta.

Roll the pasta out on a floured work surface to a thickness of about 2mm. Cut in half. Cut the first half into 1cm-wide strips, and set aside. Repeat with the second half, then cut these strips in half again so that they are half the length of the first batch. Keep them separate.

Heat a couple of centimetres of sunflower oil in a saucepan. When it is good and hot, fry about a quarter of the shorter pasta strips in it until golden brown. They will puff up a little in the heat. Scoop out the fried pasta and drain on a tray or plate lined with a double layer of kitchen paper. Repeat with the remaining short strips. Sprinkle them all with a little salt.

Return to those simmering chickpeas. The mixture should be quite soupy – if necessary add another ladleful of the chickpea water. Taste and adjust the seasonings. Now add the long strips of pasta, and stir them around a little among the chickpeas. Cook for 3–4 minutes, until just tender. Ladle the chickpeas, pasta and broth into four bowls and top each one with some of the crisp fried pasta. Eat at once, with grated cheese.

Valentina's Mother's Pasta e Piselli

Pasta with Peas and Fried Eggs

Valentina works in the little café on the corner of my street, and when she's not there she's studying for her English exams. She's one of those people who sparkles, and I warmed to her as soon as she served me my first coffee. Now we chat in a brazen blend of English and Italian. They open at 5.30 in the morning (the sweet scent of morning pastries baking sometimes wakes me up) and by lunchtime her working day is done. She heads home to Mama's restorative lunch, studying and rest.

'Today is *pasta e piselli,*' she smiles, and tells me just how her mother cooks it. I try it out that very evening. It's a classic homely dish, simple, soupy and satisfying.

Serves 4

4 tablespoons extra virgin olive oil
1 onion, chopped
1 carrot, chopped
1 stem of celery, chopped
3 cloves of garlic, chopped
40g pancetta, cubed (optional)
400g shelled peas (frozen peas are fine)
3 tablespoons chopped flat-leaf parsley
salt and freshly ground black pepper
350g *ditalini, cavatelli, ruote* or other small pasta shapes
4 eggs
freshly grated Parmesan, pecorino or *cacioricotta*

Put 3 tablespoons of olive oil into a wide, high-sided frying pan with the onion, carrot, celery, garlic and pancetta, if using. Place over a low-medium heat and fry together for around 10 minutes. Tip in the peas. Set aside a little of the parsley for a garnish and add the rest to the pan of vegetables. Season with salt and pepper. Stir everything together and let it cook through gently for a minute or two. Pour in 750ml of water and bring to the boil. Simmer together for 5 minutes, then add the pasta shapes. Carry on cooking until the pasta is just al dente.

By now the pasta should have absorbed most but not quite all of the water. If it threatens to dry out as it cooks, splash in a little extra water. If it looks too wet, turn up the heat and boil hard for a few minutes to reduce. Check the seasoning and adjust as needed.

While the peas and pasta are cooking, fry the eggs in the remaining oil over a brisk heat so that the edges brown and crisp.

Spoon the pasta and peas into serving bowls, scatter generously with grated cheese, and top each one with a fried egg. Sprinkle over the remaining parsley and serve.

Cavatelli ai Cardoncelli e Patatine

Cavatelli with King Oyster Mushrooms and Matchstick Potatoes

This started as a what's-left-in-the-fridge supper. One tray of beautiful, fat, fleshy *funghi cardoncelli*, a lone baking potato and some grated cheese. In the cupboard, a packet of pasta and a tin of tomatoes. It turns out that a small thatch of crisp-fried matchstick potatoes is a fine counter-texture to the slippery flesh of fried mushrooms, tomato sauce and pasta. It's now part of the Grigson repertoire.

Serves 4

1 moderately large potato
extra virgin olive oil
salt and freshly ground black pepper
350g *cavatelli* or fusilli
1 red onion, sliced
100g *guanciale* or pancetta lardons
250g king oyster mushrooms, cleaned and sliced, or a mix of shiitake and chestnut mushrooms
4 cloves of garlic, chopped
2 red chillies, finely chopped
leaves from 2 sprigs of thyme
10 sage leaves, roughly chopped
1 x 400g tin of chopped tomatoes
freshly grated Parmesan

Slice the unpeeled potato thinly (no thicker than 0.5cm), then, stacking a few slices each time, cut the potato into long, thin strips. Heat 3 tablespoons of olive oil in a wide frying pan and sauté the potato strips briskly until browned and cooked through. Scoop on to a plate and season with salt.

Put a large pan of well-salted water on the stove to heat up. Once it boils, tip in the *cavatelli* and simmer until al dente. Drain, reserving half a cupful of the cooking water.

Meanwhile, return the frying pan to the heat and add another slurp of olive oil. Fry the onion over a moderate heat until tender. Scoop out on to another plate. Return the pan to the heat again and add the *guanciale* or pancetta and the mushrooms. Sauté over a high heat, until the mushrooms are just cooked through. Add the garlic and chillies and fry for another minute or so. Return the onion to the pan, add the thyme and sage leaves, the chopped tomatoes and season with salt and pepper. Simmer together for around 10 minutes, adding a little of the reserved pasta water every now and then to keep the sauce moist. Taste and adjust the seasoning.

Tip the pasta into the sauce and toss everything together, adding a splash more pasta water if it looks dry. Pile on to serving plates and top each portion with a handful of crisp potato strips. Pass around the Parmesan and eat at once, while the matchstick potatoes are still crisp.

Tagliolini with Wild Asparagus, Mascarpone and Lemon

Last year wild asparagus was sprouting in the fields near Ceglie around the same time as Covid reared its ugly head. A small compensation for a big crisis. As lockdown lumbered on, slender cultivated asparagus succeeded the wild. Either works well in this recipe, which cheered me in those early dark days. It's enriched with a touch of creamy mascarpone, not a particularly Puglian addition, but delicious all the same.

Per person:
a handful of wild asparagus (or sprue)
80g tagliolini, tagliatelle or spaghetti
1 tablespoon extra virgin olive oil
1 clove of garlic, chopped
6 cherry tomatoes, quartered
1 tablespoon mascarpone
finely grated zest of ½ a lemon
salt and freshly ground black pepper
freshly grated pecorino

Put a large pan of well-salted water on to boil. Trim off all the woody ends of the stems of the asparagus and discard (or simmer in water to make a stock for soup).

When the water is at a rolling boil, add the tagliolini. Boil for as long as the packet says, minus 2 minutes (wild asparagus), 3–4 minutes (sprue). At this point, add the asparagus to the pasta and keep right on boiling for the remainder of the cooking time. Scoop out a cupful of the cooking water and reserve. Drain the pasta and asparagus.

Meanwhile, put the olive oil and garlic into a frying pan and place over a medium-low heat. As soon as the garlic begins to brown (this only takes a minute or two, so don't wander off), add the cherry tomatoes. Cook together for another 2 or 3 minutes, until the tomatoes have softened down. Add the mascarpone and a scant tablespoon of the reserved pasta water (per portion) and stir until all is melted nicely together. Add the lemon zest, salt and pepper. Tip in the drained pasta and asparagus and toss in the creamy sauce.

Eat at once, sprinkled generously with freshly grated pecorino.

Spaghetti ai Gamberi e Limone

Spaghetti with Prawns and Lemon

This is a *pasta in bianco*, a white pasta dish. In other words, it relies entirely on the flavours of the main ingredients themselves, with no scarlet tomato sauce safety net (that's *pasta in rosso*). So you need to use the very best ingredients, in this case, ozone-fresh and translucent shell-on raw prawns, sharp zesty lemons and the most vibrant, glossy parsley, and then you need to squeeze every last drop of flavour out of them. A concentrated stock made with the shells and heads of the prawns and the parsley stalks is the key.

Serves 4

800g medium-sized raw prawns in their shells
a small bunch of flat-leaf parsley
extra virgin olive oil
1 carrot, diced
1 stem of celery, diced
½ an onion, chopped
350–400g spaghetti
finely grated zest and juice of 1 lemon
salt and freshly ground black pepper

Bring a large pan of salted water to the boil. Simmer 4 of the prawns until just pink and cooked through. Scoop out, but do not discard the water. This is what the spaghetti will be cooked in. Slice the green leaves off the bunch of parsley. Keeping them separate, chop leaves and stalks roughly.

Peel and devein the remaining prawns. Set aside the raw prawns and chop the shells and heads roughly. In a medium-sized frying pan, heat a good slug of olive oil. Add the carrot, celery and onion and fry for 4–5 minutes. Now add the chopped shells and heads and the parsley stalks. Stir for another 3–4 minutes. Add 200ml of water and bring up to a rollicking boil. Turn down slightly and leave to simmer for 10–20 minutes or so, until reduced by half. Strain the mixture, pressing down to extract the last of the stock. Discard the shells, heads and spent veg. Save the stock.

Bring the large pan of salted water up to the boil again. Add the spaghetti and cook until just al dente. Drain. Meanwhile, return the frying pan to the heat. Add the stock and once it is hot, slide in the raw prawns. Simmer until just done. Add half the lemon juice, then the pasta, lemon zest, parsley leaves, a little salt and lots of freshly ground black pepper. Toss together over a moderate heat until the spaghetti is coated with the sauce. Taste and add more lemon juice or salt as required, then serve at once, topping each plateful with one of the prawns you cooked in the pasta water. Serve at once.

7

BUT WHERE ARE ALL THE COWS?

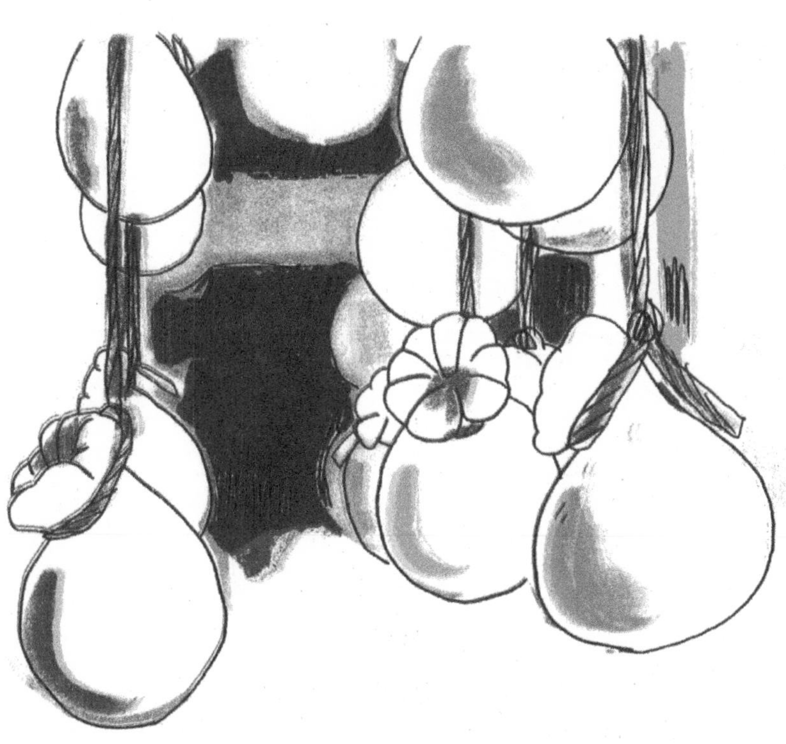

Today's new word is *solletico*. It means tickle. As in *'mi fai il solletico'* to Caterina, the beautician, as she grappled with my pedicure. Ever professional she just carried right on, as we decided that I should concentrate on something, anything, that wasn't my ticklish foot. A golden beach, planning a trip to Albania, but obviously food would provide the best distraction of all. What were my favourite Puglian dishes? And aren't the *latticini* exceptionally good? It did the trick and my toenails are now a fetching shade of burnt orange.

The local taste for *latticini*, dairy products, is a big thing. When I say dairy products, what I actually mean is mostly mozzarella in many forms, ricotta, and a gaggle of other soft cheeses. Matured pecorino and Parmesan strut proudly in their wake, followed by another bigger gaggle of semi-hard and hard cheeses fronted by *caciocavallo* and *cacioricotta*. For ages I got these two muddled until I realised that *'cacio'* is just another word for cheese. *Cacioricotta* is the hard, matured version of ricotta-like curds, though *caciocavallo* is not a hard, matured version of horse anything. Theories of how it acquired the name horse (*cavallo*) cheese abound, but I like the idea that it originated with nomadic tribes, who slung bladders of milk across the backs of their magnificent horses. Much galloping later, the warm milk had coagulated and stretched and was well on its way to becoming cheese. Wikipedia describes this as a 'naïve hypothesis'. What a pity.

Caciocavallo is, like mozzarella, a *pasta-filata*, stretched curd, cheese. It looks fabulous, hanging in drooping, bulging, football-sized (and bigger) tear-drops, from hooks and poles at the deli or the *caseificio*. Unlike mozzarella, it is a cheese that is matured for anything from 30 days to many months. Like mozzarella, it is for the most part light on flavour. I have a fondness for the splendidly monikered *schiena d'asino* – donkey's ass cheese – but honestly that's more because of the name than anything else. Although when it is cave-aged it does develop a bigger tang than that of most *caciocavallos*.

By far the best way to eat *caciocavallo* is melted. At festivals and fairs the charcoal-powered *caciocavallo* stall is a big attraction, with queues of drooling people waiting for their share of the lazy lava of molten cheese to ooze down on to toasted bread. In the failing evening light, the glow of the embers and a feeble light bulb or two silhouette the row of pendent cheeses slung from hooks over the heat. The trick, I am told, is to start them off slow, at one side or other where the lick of warmth is gentler. As the ravenous queue builds up, cheese after cheese is shunted towards the centre, to a point where the flow of rich goo is just enough for the stallholder to scrape it down on to the next slice of toasted bread, but not so speedy that he loses precious cheese to the embers.

Cacioricotta is a very different kettle of fish. Although it can be eaten young and soft, much of it is sold at a more mature stage. Once hardened to grating solidity, it becomes a bit of a thug. Very, very, very salty and lacking the grace of say, Parmesan or a good pecorino. It's fine on pasta, but when I noticed that I still had three-quarters of a little wheel of *cacioricotta* huddled at the back of the fridge, some six months after its purchase, I had to admit to myself that I hadn't liked it that much.

And the cows?

Visiting Parma in northern Italy some time in the 80s, I was overawed by the gargantuan cheese-maturing hangars with rows and rows of huge Parmesan truckles stretching up to the ceiling and to left and right into the shadows on either side. A breath-taking richness, in both senses of the word. I learnt about the strict rules and regulations laid down in law to preserve this king of cheeses. The milk, for instance, must only come from a strictly defined area around Parma, Reggio Emilia and Modena, which was precisely where I was. Why then, did I never spot a cow in the fields? Not one.

Thirty-five years on, here in Puglia I ask the same question. Apart from one small herd of long-horned Podolica cattle in the heights of the Murgia plateau, I have never seen any cows in fields. Friends tell me that they know of a few here or there, but they are not evident. The sad answer is that they are hidden from sight in vast sheds, where movement is limited to maximise milk yield. In the height of summer when the temperature passes 30°C for several months on end, I concede that this may be the better place for them, better at least than open fields with few trees. But throughout the rest of the year? Forget those happy Italian peasants tending to their happy cows mooching around grazing their lives through happy meadows. As Compassion in World Farming confirms:

'Two million dairy cows are raised in Italy, most of which currently spend their entire short life indoors, in a zero-grazing system, doing only one thing: producing milk.

'Intensive farming has replaced the natural grazing method with the practice of keeping animals imprisoned in sheds.'

That's where all the cows are.

Polpette di Pane

Bread and Cheese Fritters

My first *polpette* experience came in Zia Rosa, a small toasty restaurant in Cisternino's old town. It was a chilly night, and the restaurant was sparsely populated apart from one table. A cheery gaggle of middle-aged guys were tucking into wine and a heap of fritters. When I asked what they were, the patron grabbed a plate, whipped four of their fritters and transferred them instantly to my table. Oh, that contraband was good! The secret, he confided as his friends raised a glass to me, was to use half as much cheese as bread.

Good bread, gone stale, and good, strong, mature grating cheese are exactly what it takes to create a fine golden puff of a fritter. My friend and ex-landlady, Anna-Maria, uses an aged *cacioricotta*, which she buys from an elderly lady with only five cows to her name. Mimmo and his customers in the little shop round the corner agree that the Rodez cheese I'm proposing to use is fine, or suggest I try replacing it with pecorino, Grana Padano or Parmesan. Basically, whatever you've got, as long as it's got oomph.

You don't have to use all the batter at one go, as it will sit happily in the fridge for a day or two. Remember to bring it back to room temperature before frying, so that the *polpette* cook through easily.

Makes plenty, eat hot

120g stale bread, of decent quality
70g finely grated mature *cacioricotta*, pecorino, Parmesan or Rodez
4 eggs

2 tablespoons chopped flat-leaf parsley
1 clove of garlic, crushed
freshly ground black pepper
sunflower oil (or a mix of sunflower and a dash or two of olive oil), for deep-frying

Break the bread up into chunks, crusts and all. Soak in cold water for 10 minutes or so, then squeeze out the water and plop the bread into your mixing bowl. Beat in all the remaining ingredients except the oil. Don't add salt – the cheese will be salty enough on its own.

Use a deep-fat fryer if you have one, or if not, heat a 7.5–10cm depth of oil in a heavy-based saucepan. Slide in a test-run dessertspoonful of the batter mix and cook until golden brown, turning carefully once or twice. This should take around 4–5 minutes. If it cooks too quickly, reduce the heat of the oil.

Drain the fritter on kitchen paper, and bite into it as soon as the heat will let you. The outside should be firm with a hint of crispness, the inside tender but set, and divinely cheesey. Add more pepper, if you like. Now deep-fry the rest of the batter, spoonful by spoonful, until you have a burnished heap of golden fritters.

Polpette di Melanzane

Bread, Cheese and Aubergine Fritters

As per the recipe on page 198, but add a large aubergine to the ingredients list. Cut into lengthways slices, around 1cm thick. Brush with extra virgin olive oil and grill or roast in a hot oven until tender. Cut into small cubes and stir into the *polpette di pane* batter. Deep-fry as before.

Uova Strapazzate al Pomodoro e Formaggio

Cheesey, Tomatoey, Garlicky Egg Scramble

This is my late-night, post-drinks, what's-in-the-fridge special. A zesty muddle of satisfaction, quickly made. Naturally that means I use whatever cheese is in the fridge, sometimes a piquant *caciocavallo*, or a milder stretchy mozzarella. Mature Cheddar is even better, but don't tell my Italian friends that I said so.

Serves 1

2 tablespoons extra virgin olive oil
2 cloves of garlic, finely chopped
2 anchovy fillets, chopped (optional, but recommended)
a handful of cherry tomatoes, quartered
1 tablespoon chopped flat-leaf parsley (again, optional, but a good addition)
2 eggs, lightly beaten
salt and freshly ground black pepper
30g mature *caciocavallo* or mozzarella (or mature Cheddar), diced
a slice of toast

Heat the oil in a small (20cm) frying pan over a medium heat. Add the garlic and the anchovies. Fry for a minute or two, until the garlic is just taking on some colour and the anchovies are breaking down. Raise the heat and add the tomatoes and parsley. Fry for another 2–3 minutes, until softened.

Meanwhile season the eggs with salt and pepper. Tip into the hot pan, then scramble and scrape and cook speedily with the tomatoey goo. As soon as the eggs are just about set (it happens very quickly), take off the heat, stir in the cheese, and pile on top of the toast.

Pure milky godliness

Today, 16 August, is the festival of San Rocco, patron saint of Ceglie. In this Covid-subdued summer it is a particularly big deal. San Rocco, born French but a pilgrim through Italy, prayed for and cured those afflicted by the plagues of the fourteenth century. Last year I watched as the Saint's statue was carried through the town, lurching from side to side, to rest overnight in the Chiesa Matrice, the central church. This year he has to stay at home, and the thronged outdoor town party has been cancelled, but five ear-splitting cannon shots have just shaken the house and my eardrums. Amplified prayers and solemn music are now wafting through my open window from the square in front of the church.

It's Sunday evening, but the butcher and his staff, clad in clean red aprons, are sitting on the step, waiting for the service to end. Sausages, *bombette* and other treats are roasting in the oven, ready to feed the hungry congregation. Just around the corner, Mimmo is in his deli, slicing *cotto* and *crudo* (cooked and cured hams), mortadella and a lake of the finest, cool, tender mozzarella, ready to slip into chewy bread rolls.

It is not unreasonable to ask Mimmo or other sandwich providers for a panino without mozzarella in it, but it is not expected. Mozzarella is the essential emollient in a country where butter and mayonnaise are not ubiquitous. Good mozzarella harmonises with practically everything else you might want in between two wodges of bread. With tomato, rocket, salami, hams, other sturdier cheeses, tuna mayonnaise, pickled aubergine, grilled aubergine and red peppers, etc. etc. etc. and etc.

I have now learned to be picky about mozzarella. *Fior di latte* (flower of the milk), it turns out, is just a fancy way of saying mozzarella made with cows' milk. The best is on a par with buffalo mozzarella. What you want in either is that smooth outer skin girdling the pure white flesh inside. The centre should be soft but with a slight chewiness, milky and juicy with just a touch of acidity.

Mozzarella is the most famous of hundreds of *pasta-filata*, stretched curd, cheeses. The method is by no means unique to Italy. Greek halloumi, Oaxaca cheese in Mexico, *qashqawan* in Lebanon and Syria, and lunchbox cheese strings in the UK and USA are all stretched curd cheeses. The process begins in a standard cheesemaking way – milk is combined with rennet, curds emerge, are drained and cut. Next, they are submerged into a very hot whey bath for hours on end, which gradually transforms the curds into a stretchable mass. This big white lump is kneaded and pulled and folded and then shaped. This is where the mozzarella journey ends. Most other *pasta-filata* cheeses will then be cured and matured over days or months or possibly years.

Where I once believed that mozzarella came in just two sizes, small and medium spheres, bobbing in their bath of watery whey, I now know that these are just the entry shapes to the world of mozzarella. There are little aperitif *nodini*, knots that appear in almost every restaurant antipasto, *trecce*, larger and even larger plaits, weighing up to 2 kilos and possibly more. *Zizzona* is a mountainous breast of mozzarella. All of them so perfectly purely white and virginal.

Lia's Mozzarella and Mint Rolls

I first met my friend Lia Chokoshvili in one of my favourite shops in Oxford, Maroc Deli, in Cowley Road. It's a small, narrow Aladdin's cave of a shop, shelves packed with a glorious riot of Middle Eastern foods. I miss it. As Lia and I shuffled past each other in search of who knows what, we recognised fellow cooks. She soon began to teach me a little about her native Georgian cuisine. It was a revelation. There was a whole country's worth of delicious dishes that I knew nothing about.

Here, in a region where there is unabashed adoration of mozzarella, and where mint is included in the small roster of valued herbs, Lia's cool, pale rolls of minted mozzarella are right at home, slotting effortlessly into a hot summer's day antipasto.

The method may seem odd at first, but it is, essentially, no more than a spot of reverse engineering. Have faith, make sure the milk doesn't boil, and the rest is simple. These rolls taste best chilled overnight, allowing the simple flavours to mellow, and the texture to soften.

Don't splash out on the most expensive mozzarella for this recipe. Lia actually makes it with block mozzarella, but that's a dirty word here in Puglia. I've used a standard supermarket cows' milk mozzarella which works beautifully.

Makes 6 little rolls

250g mozzarella, thickly sliced
around 150ml milk
salt
around ½ tablespoon finely chopped mint

Put the mozzarella into a saucepan with enough milk to just cover. Heat slowly, stirring gently, until the mozzarella softens and forms one large clump. Do not let the milk boil. Take the pan off the heat.

Lift the clump of mozzarella out, letting excess milk drain back into the pan. Place on the work surface or a large chopping board. Roll out to form a large rectangle. Season with salt and scatter over the mint. Roll up tightly, then cut the roll into 3–4cm lengths. Place in a shallow dish, then pour over enough of the warm milk to cover. Leave to cool, then cover with clingfilm and chill. Serve as part of an antipasto.

Burrata

Sometimes it snows in Puglia. Not for long, not that often, not everywhere, but snow it does. This year the cold weather came late to the Valle d'Itria, bringing a few snowflakes that caught in the headlights of my car. That was in early March, just a few days before the beginning of the Covid lockdown. It was nothing compared to the pall of snow that swept across Italy in February 1956. For a month the country was repainted white from heel and toe up to northern thigh. Old black-and-white newsreels show *trulli* virtually submerged in snow, more hobbit-like than ever, and shocked locals being rescued from massive snowdrifts.

Dairy farmer and cheesemaker, Lorenzo Bianchino, was snowed in. There he was, stuck in his farm, in the hills above Andria, together with gallons of beautiful creamy milk that should have been driven straight down to the town (or turned into mozzarella, the story line is vague here). Presumably he was left with time on his chilly hands, and lo and behold he created the very first burrata.

At least that's the story I pieced together from the rather vague origin myths that surround burrata. And most of it may still be true, but the date is definitely wrong. Burrata is described with enthusiasm in the 1931 *Touring Club Italiano Guida Gastronomica*. Clearly the cheese was already well established.

The idea of filling a mozzarella pouch with a cream-heavy mix of mozzarella shreds is genius. It was probably a fresh riff on a traditional, matured *manteca* or *burrino* cheese, a *pasta-filata* pocket enclosing a ball of butter, but still genius. At turbo speed, it became a local classic and so was born the *burrata d'Andria*. Now burrata is made throughout Puglia and further afield, but the Andria burrata reigns supreme.

Burratas range widely in size and relative quality. There are small '*burratine*', weighing in at a mere 100g, or big trembling sacks of mozzarella that threaten to burst at the slightest malhandling. The larger burratas have a higher ratio of filling to mozzarella balloon, which is definitely a good thing.

There's no point getting clever with the way you serve your burrata. It has to be the star of the show, served on or with things that will just show it off to greater advantage. Make a beautiful edible bed for it to recline on like some pale, languid odalisque, wearing nothing more than a raffia choker at its neck and the lightest of embellishments.

Burrata, Pesca, Rucola e Mandorle

Burrata with Peach and Almond Salad

Serves 3–4 as a starter

1 burrata, weighing around 250g, or 2 x 150g

For its bed
20g almonds, slivered
1 ripe, sweet peach or nectarine, halved and stoned
a big handful of rocket
a small handful of basil leaves
½ a lemon
2 tablespoons extra virgin olive oil
salt and freshly ground black pepper
a few fine curls of lemon zest

Toast the slivers of almond in a small pan over a moderate heat until golden brown. Tip out into a metal, china or glass bowl and leave to cool.

Make up the bed shortly before serving. Cut the peach or nectarine into 12 wedges and cut each of these in half. Mix with the rocket and basil and two-thirds of the almond slivers. Dress with a few squeezes of lemon juice, the oil, salt and pepper. Taste and adjust the seasonings.

Arrange the salad in a shallow bowl, carefully lay the burrata on top, then scatter over the remaining almond slivers and the lemon zest. Serve.

Ricotta

I've just watched a strange short film from the 60s called *La Ricotta*, directed by Pier Paolo Pasolini, and featuring Orson Welles as a world-weary, exasperated director, filming the Passion of Christ, crosses, halos and all. The main protagonist is an extra, Stracci, a hungry local thief, desperate for food. Eventually he manages to lay his hands on a big mound of ricotta and a loaf of bread. He gorges, before being strung up on one of the crosses, alongside Jesus. Everyone forgets he is there until he eventually dies of indigestion and exposure, in front of a crowd of fashionable visitors. Hard to believe now that Pasolini was subsequently sentenced to four months' imprisonment, for 'insult to the state religion', although ultimately he was let off with a hefty fine.

Ricotta is a second-time-around cheese, made from what's left over when the main, most marketable curds have been pressed into their forms to mature. I'm guessing that this made it, way back when, an afterthought for the poor while the best cheese sold at a higher price. It is also, of course, another pure, white, mild and innocent cheese, which may have been a symbolic factor for Pasolini.

Pasolini's humble ricotta definitely has connotations of honest, rural simplicity and economy, although these days most of it is made in big pulsating machine-driven factories. Not all, though. The small dairies that cluster around every town in Puglia will all be producing their own ricotta in much the same way as it has been made for centuries, from the liquid residue squeezed out during the making of firmer cheeses. This is the whey.

In my native county of Wiltshire, and in many other cheese-producing areas of the UK, the leftover whey was fed to pigs, thus supporting a secondary pork industry. Great cheese and great bacon go hand in hand. In Italy, the whey is heated to nigh on boiling point, until little clots of white rise to the surface, eventually forming a thick crust. This is the ricotta, which will be skimmed off and ladled into plastic straining forms. Without modern vacuum packaging, it will last for just a couple of days.

Here, both in the supermarket and around the corner at my local deli, I have a choice of ricotta made from cow, sheep, goat or buffalo milk. They are all subtly different but my favourite remains the goats' milk ricotta that comes from the herd of shaggy goats that amble through the olive groves around the perimeter of the town. It's a spring-time treat, when new green grass brightens the earth under the trees, increasing the proteins and richness in the milk. Curiously, this ricotta stays fresh and sweet for a few days longer than other types of ricotta and has a denser consistency.

And finally, a quick spot of disambiguation for anyone shopping in Puglia: although *cacioricotta fresca* resembles ricotta in many ways, it is not the same thing. It's made by a different process, which also involves heating milk, hence the name. *Cacioricotta* will also appear fully matured, hard and crumbly. Spreadable *ricotta forte,* on the other hand, is a form of ricotta but is as pungent and aggressive as fresh ricotta is mild and soothing. Salted and matured for a year or more, it is much loved by locals and may become an acquired taste for outsiders if they persist. I love a reeking blue cheese but I've not yet managed to develop any fondness for *ricotta forte*. There's more – *ricotta salata* (salted and hard) and *ricotta affumicata* (smoked, usually semi-soft) – but perhaps that's enough ricotta for the time being.

Torta di Ricotta e Melograno al Forno

Baked Ricotta and Pomegranate Cheesecake

Italy, meet Scotland. Scotland, meet Italy. Baked ricotta curd and pomegranate rubies on top, crisp shortbread below. A happy marriage indeed.

Serves 8

For the base
120g butter, softened, plus extra for greasing
60g caster sugar
a pinch of salt
180g plain flour

For the top
720g ricotta
200g caster sugar or icing sugar
1 teaspoon vanilla extract
1 tablespoon cornflour or plain flour
4 eggs
1–2 teaspoons *vincotto di fichi* (see page 253) or pomegranate molasses
seeds from ¼ of a pomegranate

Preheat the oven to 150°C/130°C fan/gas 2. Base-line a 24cm round cake tin, with a removable base, with baking parchment. Grease the sides.

If you have a food processor, just whiz all the base ingredients together until they form a ball. If not, cream the butter with the sugar and salt and gradually work in the flour. Press the mixture evenly into the base of the cake tin. Bake for 25 minutes, until pale and biscuity. Leave to cool.

For the top, drain any whey from the ricotta, then beat the ricotta with the sugar, vanilla and cornflour. Beat in the eggs. Tip the mixture over the cooled base and spread evenly. Drizzle the *vincotto di fichi* or pomegranate molasses over the surface. Bake for 45–50 minutes, until just firm but still with a slight wobble in the centre. Turn off the heat, prop the door ajar, and leave to cool in the oven. Chill the cheesecake in the fridge for at least 4 hours, or overnight. Sprinkle with the pomegranate seeds and serve.

8

SUSTENANCE FOR SUMMER NIGHTS

People take evening strolls all over the world, but in Italy the *passeggiata* is a sacred rite that binds villages, towns and the whole nation together. Every evening, everywhere, is the right time to don one's finery (smart, clean, fashionable but not too quirky) and head off to the main square, the broad avenue, the seafront or wherever it is that people gather in the waning light. In summer the multitudes turn out; in autumn, winter and spring, the crowds thin to a trickle on week-nights and a small, bubbling stream at the weekend. Location and timings are intuitively understood.

I discovered the potency of the *passeggiata* back in the 80s when I studied for a brief month in the town of Perugia. That evening stroll from the Piazza IV Novembre along the Corso Pietro Vannucci to the Piazza della Repubblica, and gently back again and to and fro, became part of our daily ritual. We'd stop here and there to pass the time with new friends and acquaintances or to take a drink or an ice cream at a café. The *passeggiata* introduced us to local youth, passed on from one intake of students to the next. It was a time to try out our tentative Italian phrases on families and functionaries and a time to flirt with dark-eyed Italian *ragazzi*.

That's the joy and pleasure of the *passeggiata*. It's an inclusive thing, even when you know no one. As long as you are prepared to fold into the social fabric, to follow and observe the crowds, you are welcome. When I first arrived in Ceglie Messapica in the early summer of 2019, meandering down into the Piazza Plebiscito, the epicentre of the town's *passeggiata,* I joined the crowds and spent happy hours observing the flow and ebb from the terrace of a café, gazing over the chilled rim of a glass of Campari spritz.

That summer the town vibrated with activity almost every evening. I discovered how thrilling modern Puglian *pizzica* music is at its best when Antonio Castrignanò and his band played one June night. In July, I followed the trail of seven grand pianos dotted through the old town and piazzas, listening to jazz here and a classical performance there. In late summer an old favourite of mine, Morcheeba, rocked the town until early morning. Festivals to mark the town's favoured saints' days kept the evening streets crowded for days on end. There was a splendid food festival one long weekend, dance competitions, a battle of the bands, a weekend dedicated to outsized board games played out all around the town. Amazing.

Inevitably Covid has beaten down the exuberance of the *passeggiata* throughout 2020, but Italians don't give up that easily. Numbers are down of an evening, grand events have disappeared, but the now-masked stroll goes on regardless. The only musical entertainment in the main square comes from the man with the parrot on his shoulder's outsized loudspeaker. The first weeks of September brought noisy politics to the streets as candidates for the new mayor sold their merits to the populace. The bells in the clock tower still ring out four minutes late every quarter of an hour and there's still plenty of street food to be had from the cafés and *pasticcerie* and *gelaterie.*

Street food here falls into five main categories: fried foods, ice creams and slushies, nibbly bits, sweet pastries and the ultra-civilised *aperitivo.*

The transformative power of the deep-fat fryer is as much, if not more, appreciated here as it is anywhere else. From its magic depths come all manner of greasy delights, ready to be consumed on the go or sitting on the steps of the nearest church or fountain – *panzerotti, polpette di pane* (bread and cheese fritters) or *di carne* (meatballs), *pittule, zeppole* (sweet fried pastries filled with crème patissière), *frittura mista di pesce* (a medley of battered squid, prawns and small fish), *frittelle di verdure in pastella* (battered vegetable fritters) and just occasionally a tray of salty *patatine*, chips.

The aristocracy of nibbly bits and bobs, way more important than peanuts or crisps, are the *taralli*. My initial reaction to these little rings of crisp dough was of the so-whattish form and yet within weeks I admitted to mild addiction. I've made them myself at home, but to be honest, they were no better than the best bought ones and a right fiddly faff for something that is to be consumed nonchalantly alongside a glass of beer or wine. The dough itself is made of flour moistened with olive oil and white wine. Some versions are boiled then baked, which gives them a glossy sheen, but for me, the best are merely baked to a pale biscuit brown with a short mealy texture. The best *taralli* in town come from two tiny bakeries where they can be bought by the scoop, just plain, with chilli or pepper, fennel seed or onion, or best of all, a mixed bag to feed everyone's addictive preference.

The *aperitivo* is a genius concept. It is a drinks and canapés combo offered by virtually all bars. In the tiny Bar del Teatro on the corner of my street, it is a simple affair. At lunchtime and in the evening, a selection of small bowls appears on the counter. One contains mini *frise* (twice-baked rusks) and others may contain chopped tomatoes, chopped ham or salami, mozzarella. You just help yourself to a modest amount and tuck in. Larger bars go for something more elaborate, served on plates direct to your table – little fried *panzerottini, polpette di pane* or *carne,* mini sandwiches, ready made up *frise* and whatever else they can gussy up.

It is an undisputed fact in Italy that food and drink go hand in hand, and both are to be appreciated and enjoyed for their taste and as enablers of conviviality. In nearly two years, I have yet to see a raging drunk let alone an intimidating gaggle of off-their-head revellers here in my little town of Ceglie Messapica. To be sure, there are a few benign, garrulous, sozzled old dudes who do the rounds of an evening, handled with warm tolerance by the locals, but nothing more intimidating than that. It's a cultural thing, of course, but one that's enabled by a solid appreciation of good food on the go.

Panzerotti and Cazzatedde

Fried Pizza Pockets and Fried Pizza Dough Sandwiches

Panzerotti are small, folded over, deep-fried pizzas, which makes them perfect, satisfying, greasy street food. These days, in a tepid bid for healthier options, some *panzerotti* purveyors offer an oven-baked version, which effectively transforms it into a *calzone*.

Classic fillings include mozzarella and tomato (use the *rustico* filling on page 229), or *cime di rapa*, sausage and mozzarella, or the big whacker *ricotta forte* (wusses like me replace it with Gorgonzola) with tomato sauce to soften the impact. I love a filling of slowly cooked onion with olives and capers (use the onion pie stuffing on page 131). Ham, spinach, salami, mortadella, peas, mushrooms, anchovies, sun-dried tomatoes, aubergine – all good options.

There's a special Ceglie Messapica filling which consists of the unlikely mixture of tuna, mortadella, *caciocavallo* and capers. Interesting. If you want to be truly local, you will opt for a *cazzatedde* instead of a *panzerotti*. Basic ingredients are the same, but the dough is fried before filling, then split in half and stuffed full of whatever. Take your pick.

Makes 8

For the dough
500g strong white bread flour, plus a little extra for dusting
1 teaspoon caster sugar
10g salt

1 x 7g sachet of fast-action dried yeast or 15g fresh yeast
around 300ml tepid water
sunflower oil, for frying

For the filling
130g (drained weight) tinned tuna, drained and flaked
200g smoked *scamorza* or smoked mozzarella, diced
2 tablespoons capers, rinsed if salted
150g cherry tomatoes, halved
3 tablespoons chopped flat-leaf parsley
salt and freshly ground black pepper

First make the dough: mix the flour with the sugar and salt. If using dried yeast, mix that in as well. If using fresh yeast, make a well in the centre of the flour and crumble in the yeast. Pour in about a third of the tepid water, then use your fingers to cream the yeast into the water.

Now add enough water to form a soft dough. Knead for about 10 minutes, dusting with flour if necessary. When the dough is smooth and elastic, roll it into a ball, return it to the bowl and cover the bowl with a beeswax cloth or clingfilm. Leave in a warm place until doubled in volume.

Mix all the filling ingredients together, seasoning with salt and pepper. Divide the dough into 8. Roll each piece into a ball, then roll out on a lightly floured surface to form a circle of about 16cm diameter. Pile an eighth of the filling in the centre of each circle. Lightly brush the edge of one half of the circle with water. Lift and pull the opposite half of the dough over to cover the filling, forming a pasty shape. Pinch the edges together firmly, making sure there are no gaps.

If you have a deep-fat fryer, cook the *panzerotti* one or two at a time in sunflower oil heated to 180°C.

I don't, so I opt for a shallow fry. Pour about 1cm of oil into a wide frying pan. Place over a medium heat. As soon as the oil is hot, lay 2 or 3 *panzerotti* in the pan and fry for about 5 minutes on each side, until richly browned. Lift out with a slotted spoon and drain on a baking tray lined with a double layer of kitchen paper to absorb some of the oil. Be patient and wait at least 5 minutes before biting into them.

Panzerottini

Panzerottini are mini *panzerotti,* eaten as part of an *'aperitivo',* small bites of food served with drinks. Use the same ingredients as above but cut the mozzarella and tomatoes into smaller pieces before mixing with the rest of the filling. Divide the dough into 30 pieces, then roll out each of them, fill, fold and seal as for full-sized *panzerotti.* Shallow-fry for around 3 minutes on each side, then drain and cool slightly as above before eating.

Crema Fredda al Caffè

Frozen Coffee and Cream

In the early evening summer heat, I watch as four builders or decorators – heavy boots and grimy dusty clothes – settle down around a neighbouring table. Their order arrives. Not chilled beer or Coca Cola, not even wine or spirits, but four dainty glasses filled to the brim with *crema al caffè*, slushy frozen coffee. Their banter is noisy and robust, the *crema al caffè* is swiftly dispatched and that's it. Off home now for a shower, a change of clothes, a spot of supper and a good night's sleep.

Crema al caffè and *granita di limone* (see page 226) are the democratic coolers of choice for everyone, young or old, manual worker to high-powered lawyers, locals or summering slick northerners.

Serves 4

150ml really strong freshly brewed black coffee
3 tablespoons caster sugar
200ml whipping cream
4 coffee beans, if you have them around

While the coffee is still hot, stir in the sugar until perfectly dissolved. Leave to cool.

Whip the cream until it is a soft, cushiony mass. Add the coffee, a vigorous slurp at a time, whipping it in as you go.

If you have an ice-cream maker, freeze the mixture in that. If not, pour the mixture into a shallow, freezer-proof container and slide it into the freezer. Check it after an hour and a half. Scrape off any frozen bits at the sides and push them towards the centre of the mixture. Return to the freezer. Repeat once or twice more.

About an hour before serving, move the container to the fridge to soften.

Scrape the whole lot into the bowl of your food processor and whiz it all up into a smooth, rich slush. If you don't have a processor, use an electric whisk or mash it with a fork. It won't be quite as smooth but that won't affect the flavour.

Serve immediately, spooning the slush into small bowls or glasses and topping each one with a coffee bean.

Granita di Limone

Icy Lemon Slush

Look around the outdoor seats of any café in any piazza in any southern Italian town on a hot summer's evening, and you are sure to spot customers enjoying little bowls or glasses of freshly made lemon granita. It's slushier and sharper than a sorbet, hovering between ice and juice. There's nothing quite like it for cooling a hot soul down. Unless, that is, you opt for a *birra con granita*, beer and granita in the same glass, a miraculously restorative version of a shandy.

Serves 6

200ml freshly squeezed lemon juice (around 7–8 lemons)
100g caster sugar

Strain the lemon juice through a sieve. Put the sugar into a saucepan with 200ml of water. Set over a moderate heat, stirring until the sugar has completely dissolved and the syrup is clear. Leave to cool. Mix with the lemon juice.

Freeze in an ice-cream maker if you have one. If not, pour into a shallow, freezer-proof container and slide into the freezer. Check it after an hour and a half. Scrape off the frozen bits at the sides and push them towards the centre of the mixture. Return to the freezer. Repeat two or three times more.

About an hour before serving, move the container to the fridge to soften.

Just before serving, scrape the whole lot into the bowl of your food processor and whiz it all up into a smooth, white slush. If you don't have a processor, use an electric whisk or mash it with a fork. You won't get it quite as smooth but it will still taste wonderful. Either way serve right away in small bowls or glasses.

Teenager Alley

There's not a lot for youngsters to do here in Ceglie and there's even less now when lockdowns close the few options there were. In the balmy summer evenings they congregate in noisy groups down via Orto Nannavecchia, which is on my back-street route to the main Piazza Plebiscito. I try not to feel like I'm running the gauntlet as I stride through them, aiming instead to take an anthropological interest in the universal rituals of adolescents, and how they manifest here.

Beautiful girls, with their smooth, nut-brown skin and long dark hair that they swing flirtatiously over their shoulder, dress immaculately to show off their long limbs. Tottering on absurd high heels is not a thing here. The uneven stone cobbled streets put paid to that. Their footwear of choice is almost universally flat: pretty jewelled sandals, tennis shoes or, most popular of all, heavy Doc-Marten-style boots. Young men, bubbling testosterone, displaying a fluff of new facial hair, smoking and showing off, are still more gauche and awkward than the girls. The kings of their crowd are the guys with the mopeds. They zoom down the street, revving engines to herald their arrival and braking sharply beside their gang of courtiers. They dismount with a swagger and embrace their friends cordially, before cracking a winner's joke for them all to laugh at.

In that inevitable breaking-away mode of teenagers, they've created their own *passeggiata* tucked away from their parents and grandparents. A safe, moderately private evening space of their own, apart from the occasional curious foreigner strolling down to join the main throng.

Rustici Leccesi

Little Puff Pies with Mozzarella and Tomato

The *rustico* is a simple affair – two discs of puff pastry clasped around a filling. The classic is a mix of tomato and mozzarella, but there are plenty of variations. When freshly baked and still warm, the *rustico* is a joy, with its stretchy strings of molten cheese.

Makes 4

400g readymade puff pastry
a little plain flour, for rolling
1 egg, beaten

For the filling
130g tomatoes, deseeded and roughly chopped
150g mozzarella, diced
2 teaspoons extra virgin olive oil
4–6 large basil leaves, shredded
salt and freshly ground black pepper
4 teaspoons freshly grated Parmesan

Preheat the oven to 220°C/200°C fan/gas 7. Line a baking tray with baking parchment.

Put the tomatoes and mozzarella into a sieve over a bowl and leave to drain. Roll the pastry out thinly on a lightly floured work surface. Find a saucer or something similar with a diameter of about 15cm, and use as a template to cut 8 circles from the pastry. Lay 4 of them on the lined baking tray.

Tip your drained mozzarella and tomato into a bowl and mix with the olive oil, basil, salt and plenty of pepper. Divide between the 4 discs of pastry on the baking tray, mounding each portion up neatly in the centre and leaving a border of roughly 1.5cm all around each mound. Sprinkle a teaspoon of Parmesan over each mound.

Now brush a little beaten egg around the uncovered border of each disc. Sit one of the remaining circles of pastry on top of each mound and gently press it down around the edges, to seal in the filling. Brush the top of each *rustico* with beaten egg and bake for around 15–20 minutes, until richly browned. Cool for a few minutes on a wire rack, then eat hot or warm.

Frise al Pomodoro

Frise are Italian circular rusks, found in practically everyone's kitchen cabinet. Here in Puglia, they are majorly popular and so inevitably they come in a welter of sizes and types – tiny, medium, gigantic, classic, barley, whole grain, seeded and so on. Smaller ones can usually be eaten straight from the packet, while larger *frise* need to be dunked in water to soften. This, as I have ruefully discovered, is an art in itself. Too brief a time in water (we're thinking in and out in seconds) may be enough for a medium size, but it won't do the trick for the larger ones. Too long and the *frise* turns spongy and collapses in an unappetising mush.

For all that, they are a gem of a storecupboard essential, ready to be whipped out at a moment's notice as a snack, starter or a light lush lunch. With a handful of tomatoes, olive oil, dried oregano and fresh mint or basil, the work is done in minutes. They need to be eaten pretty much as they are made up, or at least within 10 minutes or so. If this is problematic, just put out the ingredients on the table and encourage everyone to put them together themselves. Much more fun, anyway.

medium/large *frise*, or slices of grilled bread
garlic cloves, cut in half
a handful of cherry tomatoes, or super-sweet tomatoes of whatever type
extra virgin olive oil
salt and freshly ground black pepper
dried oregano
basil or mint leaves

And when you have them to hand, any of the following:

mozzarella di bufala, burrata or *stracciatella*
prosciutto crudo
capers
black olives

One at a time, dunk the *frise* into cold water for a couple of seconds if they need it. Shake off the excess. Rub the upper surface of the *frise* (or un-dunked toast) with the cut side of the garlic. Halve one or several tomatoes, and squidge on to the surface of each *frise*, smearing them around a little. Now drizzle over a fine trickle of olive oil, season with salt and pepper, and add a good sprinkling of dried oregano. Add a slice of mozzarella or prosciutto, or a few capers or an olive to each. Top with a basil or mint leaf or two and eat.

Pittule

Fritter Puffs

Pittule or *pettole* are party food, the kind of thing you guzzle at Christmas, or on a Saint's Day, or at Carnevale, just before the Lenten restrictions set in. Little fritters of yeast batter, deep-fried until crisp on the outside, tender and puffed inside. Similar donutty things are made the world over – *loukoumades* in Greece, *lokma* in Turkey, beignets in New Orleans, koeksisters in South Africa and so many more.

Puglian *pittule* are hardly exceptional but they are very, very good. The same batter is used to make both sweet fritters and even more delicious savoury versions. So that's where I'll start, with the batter.

Makes around 24

250g plain flour
½ teaspoon salt
10g fresh yeast or ½ x 7g sachet of fast-action dried yeast
200ml tepid water

Mix the flour and salt in a large bowl.

If using fresh yeast, make a well in the centre and add a slurp of the tepid water. Crumble in the yeast, then mix with your fingers to dissolve it.

If using dried yeast, just mix with the flour.

Gradually beat in the water to form a smooth batter. Beat for another 5 minutes or so, to develop a small amount of gluten and to make sure the batter is lump-free. Cover and leave in a warm place until doubled in bulk, and full of bubbles.

Sweet *pittule*

1 quantity of *pittule* batter
sunflower oil, or sunflower oil mixed with a little olive oil, for frying
finely grated zest of 1 orange
1–2 tablespoons orange flower water
icing sugar, caster sugar, or honey

Heat a 5cm depth of sunflower oil in a heavy-based saucepan over a moderate heat (or use a deep-fat fryer if you have one). While it heats, beat the orange zest and orange flower water into the batter and line a plate or baking tray with a double layer of kitchen paper. Carefully drop small dessertspoonfuls of the batter into the hot oil, just a few at a time and fry until lightly browned, turning occasionally. Drain on the kitchen paper for a few minutes, then transfer to a serving plate and dust with icing sugar or caster sugar, or drizzle with honey. Eat while warm.

Savoury *pittule*

1 quantity of *pittule* batter
sunflower oil, or sunflower oil mixed with a little olive oil, for frying
500g tomatoes, deseeded and roughly chopped
150g olives, stoned
12 anchovies, roughly chopped

Heat a 5cm depth of sunflower oil in a heavy-based saucepan over a moderate heat (or use a deep-fat fryer if you have one). Mix the tomatoes, olives and anchovies into the batter and line a plate or baking tray with a double layer of kitchen paper. When the oil is hot, carefully drop heaped dessertspoonfuls of the batter mixture into the oil, just a few at a time and fry until golden brown on each side. Drain on the kitchen paper for 4 or 5 minutes (they are ferociously hot when they emerge from the oil), then serve.

Pasticciotti

Little Custard Cream Pies

When I announced I was moving to Puglia, my Italian friend Donatella's one key piece of advice was 'Try the *pasticciotto.*' She's a fabulous pastry chef and so, of course, was totally and utterly right. Technically it is no more than a custard tart, but rich biscuity pastry, lemony *crema pasticcera* (pastry cream) and possibly a few cherries into the bargain and it becomes so much more.

Though *pasticciotti* originate from Lecce in the south, you find them everywhere here, in cafés and restaurants and even piled high in frozen food bins at the supermarket. There are endless plays on the basic theme – some may have cherry or apricot jam or Nutella in them, and I've eaten epic apple-topped *pasticciotti.* Top prize for innovation goes to the pastry chef Angelo Bisconti, who pioneered the *pasticciotto Obama* to celebrate Obama's presidential trip to Italy – cocoa in the pastry and molten chocolate folded into the pastry cream. If anyone dares to complain about black-facing a white pastry, I shall scream loud enough to burst their eardrums.

Pasticciotti are always oval, but if like me you don't have any oval metal moulds, a common-or-garden bun tin is an acceptable substitute.

Makes 8

For the pastry
250g plain flour, plus a little extra for rolling
a pinch of salt
125g butter, or half and half butter and lard, plus extra for greasing

90g caster sugar
2 egg yolks
½ teaspoon vanilla extract
finely grated zest of 1 lemon
½ an egg white, lightly beaten, to glaze

For the crema pasticcera
250ml milk
finely grated zest of 1 lemon
3 egg yolks
50g caster sugar
30g plain flour
a squeeze of lemon juice

Optional
24 cherries in syrup or in grappa (see pages 247 and 248)

First make the pastry: mix the flour and salt. Rub in the butter (and lard, if using) until the mixture resembles fine breadcrumbs. Add the sugar, egg yolks, vanilla and lemon zest and a tablespoon of icy cold water. Cut them into the mixture with a knife, then use your hands to bring the pastry together, kneading it very briefly to smooth it out. If it is still crumbly, add a small splash more water. Form into a thick disc, wrap in a beeswax cloth or clingfilm, and chill for at least half an hour.

Now the *crema pasticcera*. Heat the milk with the lemon zest until it is steaming and very nearly boiling. Meanwhile, whisk the egg yolks with the sugar, then whisk in the flour. Pour in the hot milk, whisking constantly. Rinse out the pan. Return the custard mixture to the clean pan and place over a medium heat. Bring to the boil, stirring constantly, scraping the base and sides of the pan as the mixture thickens. Once the mixture is hot enough to burp big bubbles, cook for a minute more, whisking constantly. Draw off the heat and stir in the squeeze of lemon juice. Leave to cool, whisking occasionally.

Preheat the oven to 180°C/160°C fan/gas 4. Grease a bun tin. Roll the pastry out on a lightly floured surface to a thickness of just under 0.5cm. Stamp out 8 circles a little larger than the circumference of the bun holes. Press them into the tin – don't despair if the pastry rips, just patch it up as best you can. Fill the pastry cases with *crema pasticcera,* and top each one with 3 cherries, if using. Gather together the remaining pastry, roll it into a ball, then roll it out flat again. Stamp out 8 more circles, brush the edges with a little egg white, then lay them, eggy side down, over the cherries and *crema.* Press them down gently at the edges to seal.

Brush the tops with egg white, then bake for 25–30 minutes, until pleasingly browned. Let the pastries cool for 10 minutes in the tin, then carefully ease out on to a wire rack. Best eaten warm, but almost as good when cooled.

Chocolate

Omit the lemon zest entirely.
Replace 1 tablespoon of the flour with 1 tablespoon cocoa in the pastry.
Stir 80g of grated dark chocolate into the *crema pasticcera* while it is still warm.

With apricot or cherry jam

Half-fill each *pasticciotto* with *crema pasticcera,* then instead of cherries add a dollop of jam, and top with a little more *crema* before covering with the lid.

9

LA MIA CAMPAGNA – TALES FROM THE ORCHARD

'You follow the road to Martina Franca, keep going for several kilometres, then turn right at the lamp-post with Padre Pio painted on it. *La mia campagna* (my countryside) is on the right, white walls, green gate.'

A garden is a rarity in town. The houses are jammed tightly together, narrow streets providing shade in the summer, bowling alleys for the *scirocco* and *tramontana* winds in the winter. Communal areas among the newer-build flats encircling the old town are mostly paved, with a handful of trees for shelter. Yet the agriculturist's soul lives on through stone and concrete. Balcony flowers are not enough.

Many town families have their own essential patch of countryside nearby. My neighbour's *campagna* is typical. A couple of hectares of rich, rust-red soil, with some 50 or 60 olive trees and a medley of fruit trees to cover the entire spring-to-autumn cycle of fruit. In the centre of all this bounty is a white *lamia,* a small one-storied building that would once have provided storage for agricultural implements and paraphernalia, or possibly shelter for livestock.

Now the *lamia* has a generous terrace in front. There's a cistern for water which has to be hauled up in a bucket. The old wood-fired bread oven is well used but it has been bolstered by a new fireplace out on the terrace for grilling meat for family feasts. There are pots of bright flowers, herbs and lots of chillies, and round the back the skeleton of a double sink unit, armed with two big plastic basins for washing up. This is the only place I have ever positively enjoyed doing the dishes, gazing out across the orchard and fields, marking the tumble-down *trulli* at the far end, semi-submerged in late spring by a sea of purple periwinkles.

As the year progresses, different fruit tumble from the trees. Loquats come early, paving the way for nectar-sweet, curvaceous apricots, cherries, peaches, plums and figs, and later, as the weather begins to cool, grapes and pears and the autumnal triad of quinces, pomegranates and persimmons. A glorious, riotous progression of blessings all emanating from one small patch of countryside. It's a picture that's repeated endlessly from shore to shore, tip to top of Italy's heel.

Citrus fruits are more delicate beings and for the most part find the eastern Atlantic side of Puglia something of a challenge. They take refuge in sheltered spots in town courtyards, where they can be sure to evade damaging icy winter winds. These little oases of green and yellow and orange are a pleasure to the eye against the white walls. The perfume of the flowers in spring is sheer ethereal magic, strangely enhanced by the fumes from belching cars and ripening drains.

Lemons, oranges and clementines are far happier over towards the Ionian coast around the city of Taranto and, curiously, in a small balmy area tucked between the northern Tavoliere, the wheatfields of Puglia and the Gargano spur. The winds are softer and more caressing, the cold never quite as cold. Citrus groves thrive here, rivalling olive trees and almonds. The *clementine del Golfo di Taranto* and the *limoni Femminello del Gargano* are highly prized locally. As November progresses into winter, the piles of bright fruit in the Puglian markets swell into small mountains. Just looking at them makes me feel healthier and invigorated.

Every café, however small, offers a year-round *spremuta*, freshly squeezed juice, usually orange but it could be lemon (which comes with sugar and water for you to create your own instant lemonade just as you like it), or in the autumn, pomegranate. One Italian friend insisted that you shouldn't order a *spremuta* in midsummer – it's not the season – and she's right. By July, August, September, the oranges are old and the sprightliness of flavour dulled. Come November, as the first new season oranges trickle through, this changes dramatically. A December *spremuta d'arancia* is a big, sweet, scented, uplifting blast of life.

Cherries

When I sorted through and disposed of nearly everything I owned before leaving Oxford, I hesitated over my semi-automatic cherry stoner, a rather wonderful bit of plastic frippery. When was the last time I used it? Hard to recall. Still, on those rare occasions when I'd had a few kilos of cherries to stone, it had been invaluable. In the end it went to the charity shop and I hope that some wise soul has given it a loving home.

It turns out that here in Puglia it might have come out of its box at least once a year. Cherries are a big deal. They are the first major fruit of the year, ripening in late May and early June. The town of Turi, justifiably famous for its fat, sleek crimson cherries, holds an annual festival to celebrate their magnificence. Turi specialises in the *ciliegie ferrovia*, the Railway Cherry. This is a cherry born out of serendipity. A cherry stone casually spat out near the train rails in nearby Sammichele took root and grew into a handsome young tree. In 1935 the railway guard who lived just a few yards away realised that the cherries were something exceptional, sweet and juicy with a firm, almost crisp, texture. It didn't take long, World War 2 notwithstanding, before the new Railway Cherry was being grown commercially.

Marmelatta di Ciliegie

Cherry Jam

Cherry jam is an essential element in many local sweet pastries and in particular our very own *biscotti cegliesi* (see how proprietorial I've already become). This recipe is a compromise bilateral UK–Italy version, with the large chunks of fruit that I like in a jam dispersed in a puréed jam that is often preferred here. As a result, it is as good on a slice of buttered toast as it is in *biscotti cegliesi* (see page 283).

Makes 3 x 330ml jars

1.5kg cherries
750g caster or granulated sugar
juice of 1 lemon

Discard the stalks and halve the cherries, discarding the stones. Pile into a bowl and add the sugar and lemon juice. Stir to mix lightly, then cover and leave overnight, at room temperature unless the weather (or the kitchen itself) is particularly hot, in which case leave in the fridge.

Next day, put two saucers into the fridge to chill. Scrape the cherries with all their syrupy, sugary juice into a fairly large, heavy-based saucepan. Place over a gentle heat and stir for a few minutes to warm through. Raise the heat a little and keep stirring until all the grains of sugar have dissolved. Now bring up to the boil and let the mixture bubble sweetly for 20 minutes. Time for the first setting test. Grab one of the saucers from the fridge. Drip a little of the syrup on to it and wait for a minute or so (take the pan of cherries off the heat while you do this). Tilt the saucer gently. If the jam trickles down, then it is not ready. Put the pan back on the heat and boil for another 5 minutes or so before trying again. On the other hand, if the blob of jam stays pertly in place, it's ready to finish. If you have a sugar thermometer, the jam needs to reach a temperature of 105°C.

Turn off the heat and leave the jam for 15 minutes to cool a little. Scoop about a third of the jam into a blender or food processor and blitz for 30 seconds or so. Tip the blended jam back into the pan. Return to the heat and stir for 2 or 3 minutes. Ladle the finished jam into hot, sterilised jars (see note below), cover the surface with a disc of waxed paper, then seal tightly and label. Leave to cool before storing in the cupboard.

Sterilising Jam Jars

Preheat the oven to 160°C/140°C fan/gas 2½. Wash your jam jars and lids in warm, soapy water. Rinse well, then place on a rack in the oven for around 15 minutes, to dry and heat through. Fill the jars while they are still hot.

Ciliegie Sciroppate

Preserved Cherries in Syrup

Syrupy cherries, sweet but fresher and juicier than glacéd, are excellent in tarts like the *pasticciotto* on page 236, or spooned over a bowl of thick Greek yoghurt.

Enough for 1 x 750ml jar

500g cherries
250g caster or granulated sugar

Optional
1 vanilla pod
or:
3 strips of orange zest
or:
1 cinnamon stick

Remove the stalks and stone the cherries over a bowl to catch as much juice as you can. Put the sugar into a saucepan together with one of the optional flavourings and 500ml of water. Stir over a moderate heat until the sugar has completely dissolved, then bring up to a rolling boil. Tip in the cherries and their juice and simmer for 5 minutes. Take off the heat.

Using a slotted spoon, scoop the cherries into a hot, sterilised jar (see note on page 246), packing them in cosily. Now ladle in enough of the hot syrup to cover the cherries completely. Seal tightly and label, then cool and store in a cool, dark cupboard. Once opened, store in the fridge.

Ciliegie Sotto Spirito

No-cook Cherries in Grappa

This way of preserving cherries is just so neat and simple and satisfying. The bonus is that you end up with divinely sozzled cherries that are delicious eaten just as they are, or added to cakes or puddings, or spooned over ice cream, as well as a cherry-flavoured liqueur that will round off any meal with aplomb.

Enough for 1 x 750ml jar

150g caster sugar
500g cherries, stalks removed
200–250ml grappa, rum or vodka

Make sure your jar is properly sterilised before you begin (see note on page 246). Sprinkle a thin layer of sugar over the base. Cover with a layer of cherries, then another layer of sugar and so on until all used up. Pour in enough grappa or rum or vodka to cover the fruit and sugar. Cover loosely and leave to stand for half an hour to allow the liquid to seep right into all those little air pockets. Give the jar a gentle shake, and if necessary, top up with a little more booze. Now seal tightly and place in a cool, dark cupboard. Every day for the next 2 weeks, turn the jar upside down and return it to the cupboard. So one day it sits there the right way up, the next day it's upside down. Gradually the sugar will dissolve, the cherries' juices will bleed into the syrup and the alcohol will seep into the cherries. And that's it. Use straight away or leave for a few more months if you can wait that long.

L'Albero delle Meraviglie, the Tree of Marvels

There are fig trees everywhere and I mean everywhere. In fields and scrubland, branches spreading over the dry-stone walls, in tiny town gardens and palazzo courtyards. They seed themselves readily, springing gaily out of cracks in concrete, and even from the burlap swaddling the base of palm trees. They are tenacious, sprightly, vigorous and generous. In late summer the figs that are not harvested fall on to the red earth or the tarmac of the road, where they feed flies and wasps and get crushed by passing cars.

Down in the modern outskirts of Ceglie Messapica, opposite Unieuro, the white goods and tech shop, there is one particularly remarkable fig tree. It is huge, sprawling out across the rough grass and weeds on a patch of land surrounded by high(ish)-rise blocks of flats. I probably wouldn't have paid it much attention if it hadn't been for the large yellow plaque beside it announcing *'L'Albero delle Meraviglie'*, the Tree of Marvels.

The tree was created, quite literally, by one man, the late Pasquale Gallone. Over many years he collected and grafted over one hundred different varieties of fig on to this one tree. When you peer through the large green leaves into the heart of the tree, you can see the remains of the grafts, wrapped with black or blue tape, each one neatly tagged. As the summer heat ripens the fruit, the differences become clearer. A small white fig here, a big purple fig there, striped figs up there, some early ripening, some tardy. Each one I've tasted has been sweeter than candy, with the crunch of a thousand small seeds that makes figs unique. There are no barriers and no 'do not touch' signs.

I love this communality of figs. For a few weeks each summer roadside figs are there for the taking. Naturally you wouldn't walk on to someone's land to grab their figs, but there are just so many that no one cares if you harvest the pale green figs that hang over the tarmac, or the fruit from feral self-seeded trees. Ripe figs drop quickly on to the ground, turning from perfection to rotting in a few hot hours, so friends are delighted to pass on some of their haul to stop it going to waste.

The vast majority of the figs here are white figs, which confused me for a while as they are actually pale green, yellowing a little as they reach the peak of sugar-sweetness. Even when ripe they are small compared with the voluptuous purple figs imported from Turkey. Heavens above, they are good though.

The reason you rarely see this type of fig for sale outside home territory (and even here, few shops sell them) is that they have the keeping power of an ice cube in the desert. However many you gorge on during their short season, there are always more ripening on the tree. The happy result of this is a welter of ways to preserve them. Drying in the hot sun is an obvious option, fig jam is easy and a third option is dark, sticky fig syrup. During the centuries when sugar was an impossible luxury for most Puglians, the bountiful generosity of their fig trees must indeed have transformed them all into Trees of Marvels.

Confettura di Fichi, Arancia e Vino Rosso

Fig, Orange and Red Wine Jam

Just one of the very best of jams, with large chunks of fig in it. Next year, I'm going to make double quantities.

Makes 3 x 330ml jars

1kg ripe figs, white or purple
350g caster or granulated sugar
150ml good red wine (I use a Primitivo)
zest of 1 orange, pared off in thin strips, then cut into narrow shreds
juice of 1 orange
juice of 1 lemon
50g flaked/slivered almonds, lightly toasted, or roughly chopped toasted walnuts (optional)

Put a couple of saucers into the fridge to chill, ready for testing for a set. Rinse out and sterilise your jam jars (see note on page 246).

Quarter the figs, discarding the woody stem end. Pile into a large, heavy-based saucepan together with all the remaining ingredients except the nuts, if using. Simmer over a moderate heat until the mixture starts to look thick and jammy. Timewise this can be anywhere between 25 and 50 minutes. Stir occasionally at first, more frequently as it thickens to prevent scorching.

Grab a saucer from the fridge and drip a little of the jam on to it. If it sits proud and doesn't run, that's fine. This is a soft set jam, so it doesn't need to be perfectly firm. If you have a sugar thermometer, the jam needs to reach a temperature of 105°C.

Take the jam off the heat and let it settle for 5 minutes, then stir in the nuts, if using. Ladle into the hot, sterilised jars. Cover the surface with a waxed paper disc and seal tightly. Label, cool and store in a cool, dark place.

Vincotto di Fichi

Caramelised Fig Syrup

I remember my mother telling me how much she loathed the daily spoonful of syrup of figs she and her sister were forced to take as children 'to keep them regular'. It obviously wasn't this glorious confection.

It's not often that the ingredients list for a recipe contains only one word but here we are. Figs. That's it. Admittedly, you'll need a minimum of a kilo, which produces all of 200ml of syrup, so it's really a recipe for the owners of a fine fig tree in full fruiting mode and/or their friends. It's worth it if you have a ready supply of figs, as the dark, sweet, caramelised syrup is a wonder for drizzling over cakes and ice cream and the like, or as a glaze for duck, or in fruit salads.

Note that if you cook up a huge vat of figs, the second stage will take longer. Allow plenty of time for it.

Figs, at least 1 kilo of them

Nip the stub of the stem off the top of the figs where you need to. Chop the figs roughly and pile them into a large, heavy-based saucepan. Cover generously with water. Bring up to the boil, then reduce the heat and simmer for 3–4 hours, until the figs have dissolved into a thick wet mush. You'll need to keep an eye on it, stirring occasionally, and adding slurps of water every now and then to keep it bubbling without scorching on the base of the pan.

Put two saucers into the fridge to chill.

Set a colander or sieve over a bowl and line it with a square of muslin (or use a large jelly bag). Tip the hot fig mush into the muslin, scraping in every last drop. Leave for 15 minutes or so to cool a little. Gather up the ends of the muslin, then twist them together over the goo. Keep on twisting, pressing the juice out from the figs. Squeeze the bag hard, and then squeeze again and again and again to extract as much of the naturally sugary juices as you possibly can.

Rinse out the saucepan, then return the juice to it. Set over a moderate heat and bring to the boil. It will rise up energetically, so watch it as it heats. Reduce the heat and leave to boil down, stirring frequently. After 30 minutes, or longer if you started with multiple kilos of fruit, the syrup will have reduced by around two-thirds and will have darkened and thickened. Stir again, then drip a few drops on to a chilled saucer. Turn the heat off under the fig syrup. Wait for a minute or two, then nudge the drop of syrup with your fingernail, then pull it up a little. If it forms a short thread as you do this, then the *vincotto* is ready. If not, give it a few more minutes and repeat.

Once it is done, cool for a few minutes, then pour into hot, sterilised jars or bottles (see note on page 246). Seal tightly and leave to cool down completely before labelling and tucking away in the cupboard until you need it.

Fichi Maritati

Married Figs

Here in Puglia, foodstuffs are often 'married'. You might buy packs of married pasta, usually a mix of *orecchiette* and *minchiareddi* pastas. Or you might well buy or make your own married figs. This is a marriage of two figs, each one cut almost in half, but not quite, like a figure of eight. Before they can marry, however, they need to be dried in the hot sun, on slatted wooden racks for several days until they are stickily semi-dried. The marriage ceremony is simple; a slip of lemon zest on each side of one fig, a scattering of fennel seeds and a final benison of a brace of toasted almonds. Fig number two is laid on top and the two are pressed together in eternal companionship. Then back into the sun (or the baker's oven as it cools down) until the figs are dried enough to keep through the winter and beyond, or at least until eaten. It is a wonderful treat of a combination that binds up, in one bite, Puglia's sweetest blessings.

A Note for the Unwary

When some kind Italian offers you a perfect tree-ripened sun-warmed fig, do not, as you bite into the soft flesh, thank him or her for his/her *'deliziosa fica'* or, worse still, inform them that *'la tua fica è succulenta'*. The Italian for a fig is *un fico*, masculine. Replace the 'o' with an 'a' and you do indeed feminise it, simultaneously turning it into a slang word for the female genitals. D. H. Lawrence was right:

> . . . The Italians vulgarly say, it stands for the female part;
> the fig-fruit:
> The fissure, the yoni,
> The wonderful moist conductivity towards the centre.

Involved,
Inturned,
The flowering all inward and womb-fibrilled;
And but one orifice.

– From 'Figs', published 1923

Quince and Pomegranate Leather

Cotognata, quince cheese, *membrillo*, call it what you will, is made throughout Europe, wherever quinces grow. But I have a preference for the Arabic way of preserving fruit, in the form of thin sheets, sun-dried where this is possible, oven-dried where it is not. Fruit leathers are tarter, with a fuller, fresher flavour than a classic *cotognata*. They will keep for months in an airtight container.

This recipe marries quinces and pomegranates, whose seasons run side by side for a few weeks. The thick purée of quince and pomegranate is so delicious before it is dried that I often steal a few scoops to stir into yoghurt or to eat with whipped cream as a dessert.

Don't try to rush the drying process. You're replicating the power of the North African sun, not trying to bake it, and you really don't want to burn it. A wetter paste will take longer to dry than a dense one, so it's well worth boiling down the syrup hard to just a few spoonfuls. Just keep a careful eye on it to prevent scorching.

Makes 400–450g

1kg quinces
220g caster or granulated sugar
2 pomegranates

Wipe the fuzz off the quinces, then peel and core. Chop roughly, then put into a saucepan with 700ml of water. Bring up to a peaceful simmer. Cut a circle of baking parchment that just fits into the pan and lay it over the surface. This 'cartouche' will reduce water evaporation and help to keep the bits of quince submerged.

Leave to simmer for at least 1½ hours and preferably longer, checking regularly and adding a splash more water if needed (cartouches aren't infallible). Keep going until the cooking liquid and quinces have turned rust red. Discard the cartouche and lift the tender fruit out, using a slotted spoon. Stir the sugar into the cooking liquid remaining in the pan.

Meanwhile, line an oven tray (the big solid one that comes with the oven) with clingfilm. Halve the pomegranates and squeeze the juice out using a citrus squeezer. Sieve the juice straight into the pan of quince syrup. Return to the heat, stirring until the sugar is completely dissolved, and boil down until reduced by about two-thirds. You should end up with no more than 0.5cm depth of syrup in the saucepan.

Preheat the oven to a really low temperature – around 80°C/60°C fan/a tad under gas ¼.

Blend the quince pieces with the pomegranate syrup mixture to form a spreadable paste. If it is too thick, add a little more pomegranate juice or failing that a splash of water. If you think it is too wet, return the mixture to a clean saucepan and boil it down for a few more minutes. Then let it cool.

Spread the cooled paste out thinly over the clingfilm-lined tray. It should be no more than 0.25cm thick. Slide the tray into the oven and leave it there until the surface is no longer wet or sticky. We're talking something in the order of 8–12 hours. Carefully lift one corner of your quince leather and peel it away from the clingfilm. It should be smooth and glossy and firm. If you hit a damp patch, sigh and return the whole trayful to the oven for another hour or so.

When it is all done, spread a large sheet of baking parchment on the work surface and invert the leather on to it.

Peel away the clingfilm. Roll the quince leather up with the baking parchment. Store in an airtight container if not using immediately.

Whenever you want to serve some, use a sharp knife to cut a slice from the roll, baking parchment and all. For a shoestring strip, perhaps for a lunchbox or to serve with coffee at the end of a meal, make your slice no wider than 0.5cm. For a broader strip, perhaps for a gift, increase the width to 1 or 2cm and secure each spiral with ribbon or string.

Allorino

Bay Leaf Liqueur

The cult of the *digestivo* is a big thing in Italy, and they do it particularly well down here in Puglia. At the end of any restaurant meal, and many home ones, too, out come the *digestivi*, these potent, aromatic draughts, sweet or bitter or both. It's part and parcel of the meal-deal, a final parting gift from your host, designed to settle the stomach after a full, rich, lengthy bout of eating.

Here I should admit that although I like the idea of the *digestivo*, I'm not so keen on actually drinking them. Spirits just ain't my thing, though I'm working on it. It seems churlish to downright refuse when they are offered with a generous smile. A small quantity is all that's required, after all. So I'm sipping my way across the range, easing into the vibe. Somewhere along the way I was introduced to *allorino*, a home-made liqueur impregnated with the intense, almondy, herbal flavour of bay leaves. Oh my, how good is this new discovery!

Allorino (the Italian for a bay leaf is *alloro*) is a joyful multitasker. Sipped neat, it warms the cockles on a chilly night, but it's equally good over ice on a steamy summer evening. Of late, I've taken to lengthening it with a good splash or three of prosecco to make a Bay Royale cocktail. It slips down very easily.

It is easy to make, as long as you have access to a bay tree. You need lots of bay leaves. In Italy, you can buy 96% proof alcohol in any supermarket, sold precisely to make liqueurs like this. Vodka works well as a substitute. Two other essential ingredients: sugar and patience.

Makes around 500ml

30 fresh bay leaves (a few more or less is fine)
250ml 96% proof alcohol or vodka
200g caster or granulated sugar

Rinse and dry the bay leaves. Pop them into a bowl or large glass Kilner jar or crock. Pour in the alcohol, stir, then cover loosely and leave to macerate at room temperature. Forget about it for at least 2 weeks. A month is better.

Heat the sugar with 250ml of water in a saucepan, stirring frequently, until the sugar has completely dissolved. Leave to cool.

Strain the now beautifully green alcohol to remove the bay leaves. Mix with the sugar syrup. Decant into a sterilised bottle(s) (see note on page 246), seal tightly, label and store in a cool place for another week or two before opening.

Persimmons

My first fleeting glimpse of a fruit-bearing persimmon tree came through the window of the overnight train from Paris to Rome. It must have been early in an autumn morning. I must have been in my early twenties. Its bare black branches were silhouetted against the rising mist, with startling bright orange globes dripping from them. It signalled my arrival in the warmth and crystal light of the South.

In early autumn the leaves turn a beautiful burnt red, tumbling down as the fruit, known in Italy as *cachi* or *kaki* or *diospiri*, reach full but firm maturity. They can hang there on the bare branches for weeks without deteriorating, but are definitely not for immediate eating. *Kaki mela*, apple persimmons, are the ones you can eat while firm, like Sharon fruit, but they are far more mundane.

Biting into a mature but not yet ripened persimmon is a vile, distressing mistake. At this point in its life cycle the flesh is kept firm by a ton of über-astringent tannins that suck every last lingering drop of moisture from your mouth. *Molto allappante*, is the Italian for it. As every savvy Italian knows, the trick is to *ammezzire* your *cachi*. In other words, you need to blet or let them ripen off the tree in your fruit bowl until they feel like balloons filled with water. The process can be fast-forwarded by keeping them in a paper bag with a couple of apples, or slowed to a crawl by storing them in the fridge. A perfectly ripe, fragrant persimmon is as soft and fragile as jelly, sweet and seductive and decadent without apology.

Persimmon Sorbet or Ice Cream

Absurdly easy, absurdly delicious.

Serves 3–4

2 absurdly ripe persimmons
juice of ½ a lemon
scant ¼ teaspoon ground cardamom

For ice cream
125ml whipping or double cream

At least one day in advance, pop your persimmons, whole, on to a plate and slide them into the freezer. Ignore until frozen solid. They will keep happily in the freezer for a month or more.

Take the frozen persimmons out of the freezer and quickly cut each one into 8 pieces, discarding the calyx (the tough green part where the stem was once attached). Drop the pieces into a food processor or a strong liquidiser, add the lemon juice and cardamom and process until more or less smooth. And Roberto is your *zio*, you have the most divine ***persimmon sorbet*** which can either be eaten immediately, or scooped into a container, sealed and returned to the freezer where it will keep sweetly for a month or so.

If it's the ***ice cream*** you are after, whisk the cream lightly and fold it into the frozen persimmon mush, then eat as a sloppy semi-frozen sort of an ice cream fool, or return to the freezer to solidify for later.

Sicilian Lemon Peel Salad

Occasionally, beautiful thick-skinned Sicilian lemons make it as far as our market, or even further afield to other countries. The first time I encountered one I grumbled about the high ratio of white pith to juice, but now I know that this is something to celebrate. The pith itself is far less bitter than I'd imagined and is valued for its own unique flavour. This is the prize, not the waste.

Very thinly sliced, it makes an amazing salad that is an unexpected, simple addition to a mixed antipasto or sits well with grilled fish. Yesterday a paper-thin disc of Sicilian lemon, complete with the sharp interior, was slipped into the bresaola sandwich I had ordered for lunch. Transformational in the best possible way.

However you serve it, a little goes a long way.

1 thick-skinned Sicilian or Amalfi lemon
extra virgin olive oil
salt and freshly ground black pepper
chopped flat-leaf parsley

First pare the yellow zest off the lemon, taking as little of the white pith as possible. It's not needed for this recipe, so use it in some other way, even if only to rub around the rim of a glass that's about to be filled with a gin and tonic. Cut the lemon in half and squeeze out the juice. Cut the pith itself into paper-thin slices. Toss with a little of the lemon juice, a couple of splashes of olive oil, salt and pepper. Cover and set aside for an hour to allow the pith to absorb the flavours. Just before serving, taste a small corner and add more lemon juice or olive oil or salt. Toss with parsley and serve.

Candied Peel

Home-made candied peel is a labour of love but worth it for the zip of citrus oils that is so often dulled in readymade chopped candied peel. Any thick-skinned citrus peel does nicely – lemon, orange, grapefruit, super-pithy pomelo. Last autumn, I bought a perfumed citron from the east coast of Italy which candied beautifully. Thin-skinned limes and clementines and other mini oranges are not worth bothering with.

The first stage, repeatedly blanching the peel in boiling water, is critical to success. It draws out excess bitterness and softens the peel ready to absorb sugar without hardening. If you don't get this bit right, your peel will remain as tough as old boots throughout the candying process.

The second stage is cooking the peel repeatedly in a sugar syrup. Here it is important to make sure that a) you have enough to cover the peel itself, and b) that it doesn't thicken so much that it crystallises. Use a smaller, deeper pan to reduce evaporation. If crystals do threaten, quickly add a splash or two of water (hot or cold) and stir over a low heat until the liquid clears, then carry on without concern. Don't discard the scented, bitter-sweet syrup from candying. Add a teaspoon or two to a glass of prosecco for a candied peel cocktail, or stir into a fruit salad or drizzle over cake or a bowl of thick yoghurt.

pomelo, orange, lemon or citron peel, cut into broad strips
caster or granulated sugar

Bring a pan of water to the boil, drop the peel in and simmer for 5–10 minutes. Drain, discard the water and repeat 3 more times with fresh water. By the end of this process the peel will be much softened and translucent. If it still looks too opaque, boil it up one more time.

Weigh the drained peel, then weigh out 1½ times as much sugar. Tip the sugar into the rinsed saucepan and add the ***same weight*** of water. Stir over a moderate heat until the sugar has completely dissolved to make a clear syrup. Add the peel, bring to the boil and simmer for 4 minutes. Turn off the heat and leave the peel to cool in the syrup. Cover the pan and set aside for at least 3 hours, or overnight.

Now return the pan to the heat and repeat the simmering and cooling process. And again, and then again and finally one more time. So that's four syrupy sessions in all. If you schedule them right you can get them all done in 2–3 days. If the syrup gets too thick and threatens to crystallise or caramelise on the bottom of the pan, add a good splash more water.

By now the peel will be translucently soaked and preserved in the sugar. Drain off the syrup and store in the fridge. Spread the candied peel out on a wire rack over a tray to drip-dry. This will probably take some 3–4 more days. Store in an airtight tin until ready to use.

Italianish Orange and Walnut Mincemeat

Two British puddings have met with great success with Italian friends, largely I suspect because they both contain candied peel, a flavour with which they are familiar. The first is my mother's sweetmeat cake (see page 269) and the other is the Christmas mince pie, made with *pasticciotto* pastry, on page 271. I chickened out of trying to explain to the butcher in my feeble Italian that I wanted suet for a *dolce*, a dessert. Butter works very nicely instead.

If you have any mincemeat left over, try it in the sweet soda bread on page 141.

Makes 780g (enough for around 40 small mince pies)

100g raisins
100g sultanas
100g currants
juice of ½ an orange
3 tablespoons orange liqueur (e.g. *rosolio di arance*, Grand Marnier or Cointreau) or Strega
60g toasted walnuts, roughly chopped
100g unsalted butter, melted
60g chopped candied peel
finely grated zest of 1 orange
80g light muscovado sugar
80g freshly grated cooking apple

Soak the raisins, sultanas and currants in the orange juice and liqueur for an hour or so, until the liquid is all soaked up. Now mix in all the remaining ingredients. Spoon into sterilised jars (see note on page 246), seal tightly, label and store in the fridge until ready to use.

Sweetmeat Cake

My mother used to make this tart (not a cake at all, despite its name) for French friends to show them how excellent British cooking can be. It worked every time, and now I discover that it does the job just as well here in the south of Italy. I'm not surprised, as it is delicious, with its cargo of candied peel and toasted hazelnuts.

Serves 6–8

For the pastry
225g plain flour, plus a little extra for rolling
2 tablespoons icing sugar
a pinch of salt
110g chilled butter, diced
2 eggs

For the filling
125g chopped candied peel
60g roasted hazelnuts, chopped
2 large eggs
2 large egg yolks
175g caster sugar
175g lightly salted butter, melted

First make the pastry. Mix the flour, icing sugar and salt. Rub in the butter until the mixture resembles fine breadcrumbs. Add the eggs and mix to a soft dough. If it is crumbly, add a tablespoon of icy cold water. Knead briefly to smooth it out, then roll it into a ball, sit it on a large beeswax sheet or a sheet of clingfilm, and press it out to form a thick disc. Wrap up and chill in the fridge for at least half an hour.

Preheat the oven to 180°C/160°C fan/gas 4. Roll the pastry out thinly on a lightly floured work surface and line a 23–25cm round tart tin with it. Scatter the candied peel and hazelnuts over the pastry, then whisk together the remaining filling ingredients and pour over the candied peel and nuts. Bake for 35–40 minutes, until, as my mother wrote in her book, *English Food*, the top is . . .

. . . 'crusted with a rich golden brown colour all over, so keep an eye on it after 30 minutes. (At first the filling will rise with the baking, but once the cake is removed from the oven and transferred to a plate it will sink.) Don't worry if the centre part of the filling is a little liquid beneath the crust – it makes a delicious sauce and the consistency is a matter of taste. This is lovely eaten warm and gooey or at room temperature when more squidgy in texture.'

Bocconotti di Natale della Signora Inglese

The English Woman's Anglo-Italian Mince Pies

Most of the food that I cook here is more or less Italian, but when it comes to Christmas I'm just not prepared to jettison the traditions that I and my family grew up with. Pigs-in-blankets are essential. Stockings full of chocolate, clementines and silliness? Essential. Roast potatoes and Brussels sprouts? Essential. Mince pies? Most essential of all.

Makes 12

butter, for greasing
1 quantity of *pasticciotto* pastry (see page 236), chilled
a little plain flour, for dusting
12 heaped teaspoons Italianish orange and walnut mincemeat (see page 267), or any other good-quality mincemeat
1 egg white, lightly beaten
icing sugar, for dusting

Lightly grease the cups of a 12-cup tartlet tin. Roll the pastry out thinly on a lightly floured work surface, then stamp out 12 circles, each a little larger than the circumference of the cups. Press them into the tin – don't despair if the pastry rips, just patch it up as best you can. Gather up the remaining pastry to form a ball and pop it into the fridge while you fill the pies.

Place a heaped teaspoonful of mincemeat in each little pastry cup. Roll out the pastry from the fridge on a lightly floured work surface and stamp out 12 more circles the same size as the cups. Brush the edges of each one with a little beaten egg white, then lay egged side down over the mincemeat. Press down gently at the edges to seal. Make a hole in the centre of each one to allow steam to escape. Chill for 30 minutes before baking. Brush the tops with egg white just before baking.

Preheat the oven to 220°C/200°C fan/gas 7 and place a baking sheet in the oven to heat through. Once good and hot, place the mince pie tin on the baking sheet in the oven (this gives a sudden, intense blast of heat to the bases, helping them to cook through more effectively), and bake for 10 minutes until lightly browned. Reduce the heat to 180°C/160°C fan/gas 4 and cook for another 10 minutes. Let them cool for 5–10 minutes in the tin, then ease out and serve warm or cold, dusted with icing sugar.

Claudia Roden's Orange and Almond Cake

(with grilled nectarines, thyme and *vincotto di fichi*)

This is, of course, a Middle Eastern cake, not an Italian one, but it fits in so well here that I can't resist passing it on. I've been baking it for years and I love it just as much as I did when I first suspiciously boiled the oranges in preparation. The marmaladey scent wafts imperiously through the house, heralding good things are on their way.

The grilled nectarines (or peaches or the firm-fleshed *percoche*, a cross between apricots and peaches) are my addition.

Serves 8–12

For the cake
2 large oranges
6 eggs
250g caster sugar
1 teaspoon baking powder
250g ground almonds

For the grilled nectarines
5 sprigs of thyme
5 nectarines or peaches, stoned and thickly sliced
120g caster sugar
2 generous tablespoons *vincotto di fichi* (see page 253) or pomegranate molasses

First make the cake. Base-line a 20–23cm round cake tin, with a removable base, with baking parchment. Grease the sides.

Wash the oranges and boil whole for 1½–2 hours or until they are very soft. Leave to cool. Cut them open, remove the pips, then purée the oranges, including the peel, in a food processor.

Preheat the oven to 190°C/170°C fan/gas 5. In a large bowl, beat the eggs with the sugar. Add the baking powder and ground almonds and mix well. Then mix thoroughly with the orange purée and pour into the prepared tin.

Bake for an hour, or until just firm. Let it cool completely in the tin before turning out.

Now the grilled nectarines. Preheat the grill thoroughly. Lay the thyme sprigs on the base of a roasting tin. Scatter the nectarine slices on top, then dredge with the sugar. Drizzle over the *vincotto* or pomegranate molasses.

Grill until the sugar is beginning to bubble, then stir. Return to the grill and leave until the nectarines are slightly blackened at the edges. Stir again and leave to cool. Serve with the cake.

10

ALMONDS ARE NOT THE ONLY NUT

(BUT YOU MIGHT BE FORGIVEN FOR THINKING THEY WERE)

2019 was a good year for almonds in Puglia. 2020 was a disaster. Pity the poor almond growers, who, just a fortnight into the first Covid lockdown, watched the spring thermometer drop down lower and lower, way past normal March temperatures, and lower still until the tiny green newborn baby almonds withered and died.

Irish Brian down in the valley, owner of thirty-seven leafy almond trees, says there is not a single nut left to pick. He swears that it was the violent winds that did for the almonds on his trees, blasting them off before their time. Winds or late chills or both, whatever, the point is that one of Puglia's most important products, after olive oil, wine and wheat, is in very short supply this year. Thankfully, Brian's hazelnuts have not suffered the same fate.

You'd have imagined, then, that Giuseppe Argentiero's garage on the edge of Ceglie ('Turn right just before the Tamoil garage, Sophie') was shut and bolted this summer. It houses a magnificent nut-brown shelling machine, a Heath-Robinson-esque construction crammed into every corner. Of an average August there would be a steady trail of locals making their way to Giuseppe's back yard, the boots of their cars and vans packed to the gunnels with sacks of newly picked almonds.

They come not once, but twice. The first time it is for the

'smallatura' tunnels that loll under the shade of a tree marking the division between the neat vegetable garden (tomatoes, courgettes, massive pumpkins) and the pig run. Tacking an 's' on to the beginning of a word in Italian indicates reversing or inverting or undoing. So I *carico* my full shopping bags into the car at the supermarket, then *scarico* them when I get home. If my knickers slip from my grasp down on to my neighbour's large tub of basil as I hang the washing out to dry from my balcony, I might shout down an apologetic *'mi spiace'*, but the fragrance of sun-warmed basil on my underwear the next day will very much *mi piace* as I get dressed.

So, *smallatura* is literally the process of removing the *mallo* from almonds. The *mallo* is the soft green padding around the almond's shell. This is the equivalent of the sweet flesh of a peach or an apricot, close relatives of almonds, clinging on to the hard stone. As the almond ripens the *mallo* swells, then cracks open and begins to dry. The spiralling tunnels knock it off and it falls to the ground along with leaves and twigs and dust. Stage one complete.

Back home the almonds, still in their hard shells, are spread out on mats and plastic sheets to dry in the sun. The longer they dry, the better they keep. That's stage two.

As we drive into Giuseppe's yard, we're surprised to hear the clanking of the great shivering cracking machine in action. There's a client *caricare*-ing his car with sacks of newly shelled almonds and shattered shells (they make excellent kindling for the winter fires). He, the big brown machine and Giuseppe are just finishing stage three. The sorting screens still shimmy from side to side, channelling big chunks of shell into one chute, larger almonds (along with a considerable clatter of small shards of shell) into another and smaller almonds and shards into a third.

I ask how he has a stack of almonds to shell, when everyone else has lost their entire crop. It's a stupid question, apparently.

Everyone knows that almonds keep best in their shell, so you crack open just what you need just when you need it. These are last year's almonds. Figs are fat on the trees, plump and sweet, the sun is still hot as fire; it's time to make *fichi maritati* (dried figs filled with almonds, lemon zest and fennel seeds, see page 255) to stash away for the winter. He pays his €20 and drives off. The phone rings, another client is on his way. Giuseppe Argentiero is a busy man.

More tumbling nuts

Puglia was once a world leader in almond production, surpassed only by Sicily. Together they formed a mighty almond force. Then California happened. Essentially, the Americans worked out how to do it better. On the whole, almond trees are pretty easy-going. They like it well enough here in Puglia, coping admirably with poor soil, summer drought and winter damp. A bit of pruning now and then, a prayer or two that late frosts and winds won't take out the entire crop, and that's about it. No need to irrigate, which is a blessing in a land where summer rains are sparse. Meanwhile, the peachy-keen new almond farmers of Sacramento Valley did try irrigation and were swiftly rewarded with bumper crops. By the mid-1960s Puglia was a forgotten backwater in the world of nuts.

For all this doom and gloom, almonds remain hugely important here, even if some are trucked over from Sicily or even flown in over the Atlantic. In my little town, there are several shops that specialise in *dolci di mandorle*, almond-based biscuits and sweets. Many are delicious (I'm still begging for the *limoncini* recipe), some are dull, dull, dull. I've yet to see anything approaching the stunning displays of painted marzipan fruits and animals that you find in Palermo, which bothers me not a jot, as I've never cared for marzipan anyway.

Friends tell me that Easter brings out the artists in cooks and children in the form of the Paschal lamb, sculpted in home-made marzipan, stuffed with Nutella or jam, then primped and painted. They are, says Wendy, quite disturbing. I imagine that the Christmas marzipan fishes fall into the same category.

Ingredient note

I searched local supermarket shelves in vain for ground almonds. It's not that they don't exist in larger shops, it's just that round here everyone expects to grind their own, not so surprising for an area that traditionally grows shedloads of almonds. Although you could make the Rosata almond cake with ready-ground almonds, the texture and flavour would be diminished. Under no circumstances whatsoever should the *biscotti cegliesi* be attempted with ready-ground almonds.

Whether to grind your almonds brown-skin on or blanched is another decision to be made. The skins add an extra depth of flavour, speckling the cake or biscuit with a rosy tint. On the other hand, they make for a slightly drier texture overall. Either way, grind them carefully, scraping around the sides and the base of your food processor (or mortar if you head down a more traditional route) between bursts of action, to break up tightly compacted oily deposits.

Rosata di Mandorle

Almond Cake

This is one of those rare and happy cakes that tastes better the day after it's made. The flavours mellow and blend, but the almonds keep it moist and fragrant. I love the plain version with no more than vanilla and a (generous) dash of liqueur, but you can gussy the whole affair up with chocolate drops if you long for something more indulgent.

Grinding your own skin-on almonds is key to maximising the almondiness and lots of little nubbles of nut amid the tender body of the Rosata.

Serves 8–12

a little oil or butter for greasing the tin
200g almonds in their skins (or you can use blanched almonds)
120g caster sugar
30g plain flour (gluten-free works fine here)
4 eggs, separated
1 teaspoon vanilla extract
3 tablespoons Strega (or other liqueur)
1 teaspoon lemon juice
a pinch of salt
icing sugar, for dusting (optional)

Optional
80g dark chocolate, chopped, or dark chocolate drops
or:
finely grated zest of 1 lemon (and replace the Strega with limoncello or gin)

or:
finely grated zest of 1 orange (and replace the Strega with Grand Marnier or Cointreau)

Preheat the oven to 180°C/160°C fan/gas 4. Base-line a 24cm shallow springform cake tin with baking parchment and grease the sides.

Tip the almonds into the bowl of your food processor and add 3 tablespoons of the caster sugar. Grind as finely as you can. Mix with the flour.

Whisk the egg yolks with the remaining sugar, the lemon or orange zest, if using, and the vanilla extract until thick and light and pale. Use an electric whisk if you don't want your arms to wilt beyond use. Whisk in the liqueur. Wash your whisk well to remove all traces of egg yolk.

Now, in a separate bowl, whisk the egg whites with the lemon juice and salt until they form soft peaks. Fold alternate scoops of the almonds and the egg whites into the egg yolks until all are nicely blended. Pour into the prepared cake tin. Scatter the chocolate, if using, over the batter. Bake for around 30 minutes, until golden brown. Test by plunging a skewer or cocktail stick into the centre. When it comes out clean, the cake is done. Cool in the tin before unmoulding.

If you want a tad more glamour, dust with icing sugar before serving.

Biscotti Cegliesi

Almond Biscuits

These chunky almond biscuits (*u pesquett* in local dialect) are the pride of my new home town. At the end of a meal at nearly every restaurant, the waiter comes out with a couple of bottles of liqueur or *amaro*, often home-made, and a little plate of *biscotti cegliesi*, all included in the price of the meal. It's a charming touch.

The Biscotto di Ceglie Messapica even has its own Consorzio Tutela, the local producers' safeguarding consortium, dedicated to preserving its authenticity. The real deal has to be made with locally-grown almonds and a sticky sweet orange liqueur called *rosolio di agrumi*, but you can turn out a damn fine version without either.

Sometimes the biscotti are coated in a sugary chocolate glaze. Frankly I think this is a mistake.

Biscotti cegliesi keep beautifully in an airtight container for 4 or 5 days.

Makes 10

250g blanched almonds
75g caster sugar
1 tablespoon runny honey
1 teaspoon Strega or sweet orange liqueur
finely grated zest of 1 lemon
1 medium egg, lightly beaten
3 tablespoons cherry jam

Preheat the oven to 180°C/160°C fan/gas 4. Line a baking tray with baking parchment.

Spread half the almonds out on a baking tray and toast in the oven for 5–10 minutes, until golden brown. Cool.

Process the toasted and untoasted nuts together until they are fairly finely ground but still with a few knobbles. Tip into a bowl and add the sugar, honey, Strega, lemon zest and egg. Mix to a soft dough.

Turn out on to your work surface and knead the dough for a couple of minutes to smooth it out. Lay a large square of baking parchment or greaseproof paper in front of you. Press and pat the almond dough out on it to form a square, roughly 15cm x 15cm. Spoon the jam in a line across the middle, from edge to edge. Using the baking paper to help you, lift one side of the square and roll it over to cover the jam. Turn and repeat with the opposite side, moulding the dough over the jam so that it is hidden in the centre. Do not panic if the dough splits, or if jam comes through here or there. Patch things up as best you can and carry on.

Still in its paper jacket, roll the log of dough back and forth to form a long sausage approximately 3cm, or slightly less, in diameter. Unroll, trim off the ends, then cut the sausage into 10 pieces. Lift them on to the prepared baking tray. Reshape them gently if need be. Bake for 15–20 minutes, until golden brown. Cool for 5 minutes or so on the tray, then move to a wire rack to finish cooling.

Mandorle Atterrate

Chocolate and Almond Bites

Mandorle atterrate are the Puglian equivalent of chocolate Rice Krispie cakes, and require about the same level of skill. I've added some candied peel to the basic chocolate almond combo, but that's entirely optional.

equal weights of blanched almonds and dark or milk chocolate
chopped candied peel, as much as you like

Preheat the oven to 200°C/180°C fan/gas 6. Line a baking tray with baking parchment.

Spread the almonds out on a separate baking tray and toast in the oven for 5–10 minutes, until golden brown (keep checking every 2 minutes or so). Let them cool until tepid or cold.

Break the chocolate up into small pieces, then melt over a pan of gently simmering water, or in the microwave. Stir in the almonds and candied peel. Dollop dessertspoonfuls of the mixture on to the parchment-lined tray and leave to cool and set. Pile them into an airtight tin and store in the fridge if the weather is hot, or the cupboard if not. And that's about it.

La Cupeta

Almond Lemon Brittle

200g blanched or skin-on almonds
300g caster or granulated sugar
50g honey
finely grated zest of 1 lemon
1 teaspoon flaky salt, crumbled a little

Preheat the oven to 200°C/180°C fan/gas 6. Line a baking tray with baking parchment.

Toast the almonds on a separate baking tray in the oven for 5–10 minutes, checking regularly, until golden brown (blanched almonds) or a couple of shades darker (skin-on almonds). For this recipe, you can use them hot from the oven or cool.

Make a caramel (see below) with the sugar, honey and 4 tablespoons of water. Tip in the nuts, lemon zest and salt, take off the heat and stir briefly until the nuts are all coated in caramel. Tip out on to the parchment-lined baking tray and spread out to a thickness of no more than 1cm. Leave until tepid, then cut into squares or fingers. Cool completely. Store in an airtight container, separating the layers with sheets of baking parchment to stop them sticking together.

Note

Making caramel: I don't want to put you off making *cupeta* but I need to confess. I really hate making caramel. I've had so many disasters over the years, even though technically I know just how to do it. When it works, and sometimes when it doesn't, it tastes so good that I forget the misery until the next time. Sort of like childbirth, but a lot less painful.

It's just a pile of sugar, folks. And some honey, in this case. So, here we go. Ideally, you will use a heavy-based saucepan with a white or pale interior. That way you can see the colour of the sugar syrup more clearly. Pile in the sugar, honey and a few tablespoons of water. The exact amount is not important. 4 or 5 tablespoons are generally enough, unless you are making industrial quantities of caramel. If you add more, the sugar will dissolve more speedily, but the syrup will take longer to caramelise. If you add too little, the sugar may not dissolve perfectly, and the syrup is more likely to suddenly seize up and crystallise.

Place the pan over a low to moderate heat. Stir continuously to help dissolve the sugar. Keep on stirring, and scraping down sugar crystals stuck to the sides. Do not let it boil. After a few minutes, clamp a lid on tightly and leave to finish dissolving for a minute or so. The steam that condenses on the underside of the lid then drips down to wash lingering sugar crystals into the syrup.

As soon as you have a perfectly clear, crystal-free syrup, stop stirring, raise the heat, and gently swirl the pan to even out the heat. Watch carefully until the syrup turns a rich, nutty brown colour. Whip off the heat and use as required.

If calamity strikes and the syrup crystallises before it caramelises, panic not. Reduce the heat, add more water, re-dissolve the sugar and carry on as normal.

If the caramel crystallises as you stir in the nuts, just carry right on. The brittle will turn out like a classic Louisiana praline, opaque and delicious. Just don't let on that the caramel was meant to resemble clear amber wrapped around those beautiful almonds.

Latte di Mandorle

Almond Milk

This is my summer crush, in both senses of the word. Home-made almond milk is so so so much more than the ready made stuff from cartons. Miraculously rich and light and refreshing all at once, with a pure almondy flavour. Just joyous.

Although it is a traditional Puglian drink, the sad thing is that most bars these days just pour it straight from a cash 'n' carry carton. You might just as well be in a Starbucks in Bognor Regis.

I like it best with the gentle waft of lemon zest in it, but if you want to play with the taste, replace it with orange or lime zest, or even a teaspoon or two of orange flower water. Or just keep it simple with nothing but almonds, sugar and water. I've also tried it with a dash of honey or maple syrup replacing the sugar. All good, but this is the version I come back to in the end.

Makes around 1 litre

50g caster or granulated sugar
1 litre hot water
200g blanched whole almonds
finely grated zest of 1 lemon

Stir the sugar into the hot water until completely dissolved. Put the almonds and lemon zest into a food processor or liquidiser. Add about a quarter of the sugar water and whiz it up until the almonds have been crushed right down. Now add the remaining sugar water and give it all one last blast.

Line a large bowl with a clean tea towel or a double layer of muslin. Pour in the almond mixture. Give it a bit of a stir, then set aside at room temperature for about an hour. Gather up the ends of the cloth and twist and squeeze out every last drop of almond milk. Stir again, then chill. Stir again right before serving, then pour. That's it, ready to drink. The almond milk will keep in the fridge for 3–4 days.

P.S. Those pale, leftover, wrung-out almond grounds . . . seems a shame to chuck them out, but to be frank they taste of precious little. Ignore anyone who says they can be used instead of ground almonds in cakes or puddings. There's no benefit to be had there. Texture is all that's left. I have on occasion worked them into bread dough, where they add a mildly pleasing knobbliness to the finished loaf. Otherwise tip them firmly into the food waste bin.

Caffè Leccese

Iced Almond Milk Coffee

Long before almond milk became a 'dairy alternative', the cafés of the baroque town of Lecce were assuaging their customers' summer thirst with glasses of iced *caffè leccese*, a strong espresso coffee topped up with almond milk, over clinking cubes of ice.

Serves 1

large ice cubes (so they don't melt too quickly and dilute the drink)
1 espresso coffee
almond milk

Clink some ice cubes into a glass. Tip in the espresso and then add as much almond milk as you like. Or do it the other way round. Personally, I go for a 50/50 mix, but I like my coffee quite strong.

Shadows

In hot countries shadows are precious. August, walking back from the market, too close to midday, I seek them out, zig-zagging my way home. Even in the narrow streets of the old town, the shadows are fast disappearing and the sun hangs overhead. I'm envious of the cats and dogs curled up in shady margins, semi-comatose in the heat. The wariest of them barely open their eyes as I pass. Shadow washing swings on the pavement. The silhouette of a papyrus plant sways for a second or two in a benign breeze that's gone too soon.

Pistacchi

Piss-ta-key. Two 'c's, no 'shh' sound, no 'o' and no 's' – I still find it hard to get my head around the pronunciation of pistachios in Italian. Looked at from this perspective, it's lucky that they don't feature largely in Puglian cooking. Naturally, the *gelaterias* sell excellent pistachio ice cream. Occasionally, a restaurant gets all fancy and builds a pistachio pesto into their menu; another mistake, in my opinion, but it seems to go down well enough.

Sicily lords it over the rest of Italy when it comes to pistachios. The town of Bronte, nestling at the foot of Mount Etna, is rightly famous for its pistachios, grown in the fertile lava soils. Over in Basilicata, the province that borders Puglia to the west, there's a small oasis of well-ordered modern pistachio cultivation around the town of Stigiano. Pistachios can be grown successfully in Puglia, but few farmers are interested in taking a commercial risk with them. It takes some five to six years for a young pistachio tree to start producing a decent crop of nuts, and for most that's just too long.

Oriel's Fig, Ricotta and Pistachio Salad

Life happens, dear friends drift off into other worlds and suddenly it's thirty years since you last saw them. To my amazement, I discovered quite by chance that my long-lost friend, Oriel, was living nearby. Decades ago, holidaying with her in Sardinia, we created a 'traditional' local dish of barbecued figs and pistachios, which I passed on to my mother, then the *Observer* food writer. She bought it hook, line and sinker. In the end, I lost my nerve and fessed up before it appeared in print.

Figs and pistachios appeared again in Oriel's Puglian kitchen this time around, along with a mound of fresh ricotta. 'Can you make a salad with that?' she asked, so I did and this is it.

Serves 6

6 ripe purple figs, or 12 ripe green figs
2 handfuls of rocket
2 tablespoons balsamic vinegar
4 tablespoons extra virgin olive oil
salt and freshly ground black pepper
150g ricotta
20g roughly chopped pistachios
4–6 plain or fennel seed *taralli* (see page 219) or a crisp olive oil breadstick, roughly crumbled (optional)
a small handful of basil

Quarter purple figs or cut green figs in half. Make a bed of rocket on a serving dish and arrange the figs on top. Drizzle the balsamic vinegar and olive oil generously over them.

Season with salt and pepper. Scoop out dessertspoonfuls of ricotta and dot them around among the figs. Scatter over the pistachios and the *taralli* crumbs, if using. Pull the basil leaves off their stems and strew them artfully here and there, then serve.

Dolcetti di Pistacchi

Soft Almond and Pistachio Biscuits

Ceglie's Caffè Centrale dates back to 1861, and still specialises in *prodotti artigianali di mandorle,* handmade almond products. In among them the green of the *dolcetti di pistacchi* stands out. This is my tribute to the young couple who work ceaselessly to keep their customers sweet.

These little biscuits are simple to make and a joy to eat with their moist interior and gentle waft of pistachio and lemon.

Makes 20

100g shelled pistachios
150g icing sugar, plus extra for rolling
100g ground almonds
finely grated zest of 1 lemon
a pinch of salt
1 egg white, lightly beaten

Blitz the pistachios with the icing sugar until they are fairly finely ground. Mix with the almonds, lemon zest and salt in a bowl. Add the egg white and mix until you have a soft dough. Knead briefly to smooth out, then wrap loosely in baking parchment and chill in the fridge for 1 hour to firm up.

Preheat the oven to 180°C/160°C fan/gas 4. Line a large baking tray with baking parchment.

Dust the work surface with icing sugar. Divide your dough in two. Roll each piece out to form a plump sausage, 2–3cm in diameter. Cut each sausage into 10 pieces. Round the corners and even up each piece with your fingers, to form a thick disc. Turn the base and top in icing sugar, and place on the prepared baking tray.

Bake for 10–12 minutes. The biscuits are done when they have cracked here and there, but they should not be brown. Cool on the tray for a few minutes until they firm up, then move them on to a wire rack to lose the rest of their heat.

Those that aren't eaten straight away can be stored in an airtight tin.

Nocciola – A Nut of Little Importance

Despite a plenitude of hazel trees dotted around the countryside, and a small but not negligible commercial production, hazelnuts don't get much of a mention on menus, or in Puglian cookery books or cookery videos. I guess they are just second best to the magical almond, fount of so many sweet delights, present at every celebration in one form or another. I, on the other hand, adore hazelnuts, especially when roasted to a rich, sweet toastiness. Paired with basil and a touch of chilli in pesto, or in cakes and puddings, they bring something that the more subtle almond lacks.

Like pistachios, the one place they find a happy home is at the *gelateria*, where I was recently introduced to the *caffè nocciola* – a shot of hot, dark espresso coffee poured over a scoop of hazelnut ice cream. I never take sugar in my coffee, but this blend of melting, creamy, hazelnutty sweetness and dark, bitter coffee was a dose of pure unadulterated pleasure.

Hazelnut Pesto

Pesto proper is a northern Italian thing, from Liguria and the town of Genoa. Here in the south, it's probably made and used far less than in your average middle-class British kitchen. As an average British expat, however, I hold fast to the notion that when you have a lot of basil growing with unstinted vigour on your balcony, pesto is the obvious answer to practically everything. Pine-nuts barely get a look-in down here, but toasted hazelnuts work well instead.

This pesto has a touch of Puglian energy in the form of a handful of mint, and just a little teensy bit of chilli.

Enough for 4 people, on pasta

around 50g basil leaves
around 10g mint leaves
40g hazelnuts, toasted and skinned if necessary
2 cloves of garlic, roughly chopped
½ a green chilli, deseeded and roughly chopped
40g freshly grated Parmesan or pecorino, or a mix of the two
a little salt
around 100–120ml extra virgin olive oil

How much do you want to channel your inner *nonna*? If the answer is 'not a lot', then use a food processor for this. If she's screaming to get out, grab a pestle and mortar, ignore her protests that this is not traditional pesto as made in Genoa, and start grinding.

No-*nonna* processor method: pack the basil and mint leaves into the processor bowl first, then add all the other ingredients except the oil. Process until very finely chopped, then slug in the olive oil, bit by bit, scraping down the sides once or twice, until you have a thick, creamy pesto.

Inner-*nonna* method: check your mortar. If the inside is smooth and sleek, put it back into the cupboard and revert to the food processor method. A good mortar should be just rough enough to grip the ingredients as they grind down. Tip in the hazelnuts, garlic, chillies and a pinch of salt. Now grind, i.e. move the pestle around in a circular motion, so that the ingredients are crushed between the curve of the pestle and the curve of the bowl. The occasional thump of heavy-handed pounding to break up a stubborn lump is fine, but it's that circular motion that really does the work. Scrape the pasty nut/garlic mixture off the sides, breaking it up a little. Now add a big handful of the herb leaves. Grind these down, then add more leaves, repeating until they are all incorporated. Work in the olive oil, then stir in the cheese. Done.

Any unused pesto can be stored in a clean jar, with a thin film of olive oil over the surface to prevent discoloration, in the fridge for up to 3 or 4 days. It also freezes well.

Torta di Cioccolatto e Nocciole

Dark Chocolate and Hazelnut Cake

I have been a little obsessed with this cake since first taste, not here in Italy, but in a kitchen in Oxford. It's dark, dense and not too sweet. Definitely a grown-up's chocolate cake. The original recipe came from a book on Italian food, but which book by which author is lost in kitchen mists. I apologise to the unknown writer. I've tweaked it here and there, adding olive oil, ignoring the self-raising flour, but I cannot claim it as my own.

The famous *gianduja* mix of chocolate and hazelnuts is a northern Italian thing, but pretty much every Italian considers Signor Ferrero, father of Nutella, a national hero. So much so that in 2014 the Italian Post Office issued a commemorative stamp on the 50th anniversary of Nutella's creation. The iconic jar of Nutella, against a golden backdrop, flew the length and breadth of the country in a speeded-up version of its original national conquest.

Anyway, the point is that this cake goes down very well here in Puglia, with both Italian locals and us interlopers alike.

Serves 8–12 generously

150g hazelnuts, toasted, skinned and roughly chopped
3 rounded tablespoons cocoa
90g plain flour
1 level teaspoon baking powder
150g lightly salted or unsalted butter, softened, plus a little extra for greasing

100ml extra virgin olive oil
185g light muscovado sugar
4 eggs

To serve
icing sugar
a little more cocoa

Preheat the oven to 180°C/160°C fan/gas 4. Base-line a 23cm springform cake tin with baking parchment and butter the sides.

Mix the hazelnuts, cocoa, flour and baking powder. In a separate bowl, cream the butter, olive oil and muscovado sugar together until the sugar has completely dissolved. Now beat in the first egg, followed by a big scoop of the hazelnut mixture. Repeat with the remaining eggs and hazelnut mixture.

Scrape all the mixture into the prepared cake tin and bake for 35–45 minutes, until firm. Check that the centre is cooked through by sticking a skewer into the heart of the cake. If it comes out clean, then it is done. Cool for 20 minutes in its tin, then unmould and let the cake finish cooling on a wire rack.

Dredge the top lightly with icing sugar. Place a down-turned cup or glass in the centre, then dust lightly around it with a little cocoa. Lift off the cup/glass to reveal a white circle in the centre, then serve, before an unruly breeze wafts in to ruin your artwork.

ACKNOWLEDGEMENTS

Thank you everyone.

Thank you William Shaw for keeping the idea for the book alive and for decades of beautiful photographs, for four companionable October days of Puglian snapping, and for putting the new bed together while I cooked.

Thank you Florrie Grigson and Sid Black for support, warmth, laughter, joy. It has been the biggest honour and pleasure of my life to see you becoming the remarkable adults you are now.

Grazie Maria Altavilla per la tua generosità, i tuoi caffè e il tuo cibo meraviglioso.

Grazie Bar del Teatro, Innamorata, Movida, Montpelier per tutti i deca doppi macchiati.

Thank you Heather Holden-Brown for taking me on again after such a long break, for telling it like it is and for your warmth and support.

Grazie Annamaria Buffana, Vito Amico, Martina e Giovanni per la vostra amicizia e per avermi ospitata nella vostra prima casa.

Thank you Lindsey Evans, Kate Miles and the team at Headline for your interest and enthusiasm and for transforming my ramblings into a beautiful book.

Thank you Kavel Rafferty for drawing such elegant, un-schmaltzy illustrations.

Grazie Erika de Filippo and Ettore Condorelli for the hours you spent encouraging me to speak Italian and to dare to make the break from Oxford.

Grazie again to Erika for correcting my many Italian errors in the manuscript.

Grazie mille a tutti!

INDEX

agnello ai piselli e limone 68–9
agretti 15
Oven-cooked Agretti Frittata 47–8
allorino 260–1
almonds 277–80
Almond Biscuits 283–4
Almond Cake 281–2
Almond Lemon Brittle 286–7
Almond Milk 288–9
Burrata with Peach and Almond Salad 209
Chocolate and Almond Bites 285
Iced Almond Milk Coffee 290
Orange and Almond Cake 273–4
Soft Almond and Pistachio Biscuits 294–5
Squash Caponata with Raisins and Toasted Almonds 23–4
Altamura 119–20
Altamura-style Bread 122–3
anchovies: Fritter Puffs 234–5
Andria 207
aperitivi 218, 219, 223
Argentiero, Giuseppe 277–9
artichokes 34
Artichoke Fritters 36–7
Artichoke and Prawn Salad 38–9
preparing 34–5
asparagus 42–4
Tagiolini with Wild Asparagus, Mascarpone and Lemon 188–9
Wild/Sprue Asparagus Frittata 45–6
aubergines: Aubergine Pickles 152–3
Bread, Cheese and Aubergine Fritters 200
Cavatelli Pasta with Bread Fritters and Aubergine in Tomato Sauce 167–9
Sweet-sour Aubergine with Tomato, Olives and Capers 21–2
barba di frate see agretti
Bari 76, 84, 95, 108, 126, 133, 162
focaccia barese 126–7
basil 8
chipotle basil mayonnaise 105–7
Hazelnut Pesto 297–8
bay leaves 8
Bay Leaf Liqueur 260–1
beans: Bean Purée with Bitter Greens 51–2
and pasta 178
beef: Beef and Red Wine Stew 66–7
Meatballs 59–60
Mozzarella-stuffed Meatloaf 63–5
Slow-cooked Beef or Veal Rolls in Tomato Sauce 175–7
beeswax cloths 8–10
Bianchino, Lorenzo 207
Bisconti, Angelo 236
biscotti Cegliesi 283–4
biscuits: Almond Biscuits 283–4
Soft Almond and Pistachio Biscuits 294–5
bocconotti di natale della signora inglese 271–2
bombette 61–2
brasciole al sugo 175–7
bread 117–21
Altamura-style Bread 122–3
Bread, Cheese and Aubergine Fritters 200
Bread and Cheese Fritters 198–9
Cavatelli Pasta with Bread Fritters and Aubergine in Tomato Sauce 167–9
Craggy Tomato and Olive Rolls 137–9
'Crumbless' Flattish Sandwich Breads 135–6
focaccia 124–5
focaccia barese 126–7
Italian Spotted Dog 141
Potato and Rosemary Focaccia 128–30
pucce 133–6

breadcrumbs: Puglian Fried Peppers with Breadcrumbs and Capers 30–1
Brindisi 84–5
broad beans: Bean Purée with Bitter Greens 51–2
broccoli: Orecchiette with Bitter Greens 165–6
burrata 207–8
  Burrata with Peach and Almond Salad 209
burrata, pesca, rucola e mandorle 209
buttermilk: Italian Spotted Dog 141
butternut squash: Squash Caponata with Raisins and Toasted Almonds 23–4

Caccetta, Giovanni 133
caciocavallo 195–6
  Cheesey, Tomatoey, Garlicky Egg Scramble 201–2
  Little Pork, Pancetta and Cheese Parcels 61–2
  Pasta Gratin with Meatballs 170–2
cacioricotta 195, 196, 211
  Bread and Cheese Fritters 198–9
  Oven-cooked Agretti Frittata 47–8
  Parsley and Mint Frittata 49–50
caffè leccese 290
caffè nocciola 296
cakes: Almond Cake 281–2
  Dark Chocolate and Hazelnut Cake 299–300
  Orange and Almond Cake 273–4
Candela 3, 4, 6
candied peel 265–6
  Chocolate and Almond Bites 285
  Italianish Orange and Walnut Mincemeat 267–8
  Sweetmeat Cake 269–70
cane macchiato 141
capers 18–19
  Puglian Fried Peppers with Breadcrumbs and Capers 30–1
  Sweet-sour Aubergine with Tomato, Olives and Capers 21–2
caponata 19–22
  caponata di zucca rossa 23–4
caramel: Almond Lemon Brittle 286–7
carciofi fritti 36–7
cavatelli 162–3
  Cavatelli with King Oyster Mushrooms and Matchstick Potatoes 186–7
  Cavatelli Pasta with Bread Fritters and Aubergine in Tomato Sauce 167–9
cavatelli ai cardoncelli e patatine 186–7
cavatelli con polpette di pane, melanzane e sugo 167–9
cazzatedde 221–3
Ceglie Messapica 4, 7, 70, 146, 241
  biscotti Cegliesi 283–4
  Caffè Centrale 294
  festival of San Rocco 203
  figs 249
  Forno di San Lorenzo bakery 128
  Macelleria da Franco 57–8
  market 13–14
  panzerotti and *cazzatedde* 221–3
  passeggiata 217–18, 228
  shadows 291
  teenagers 228
cheese 195
  Baked Ricotta and Pomegranate Cheesecake 212–13
  Bread, Cheese and Aubergine Fritters 200
  Bread and Cheese Fritters 198–9
  burrata 207–8
  Burrata with Peach and Almond Salad 209
  caciocavallo 195–6
  cacioricotta 195, 196, 211
  Cheesey, Tomatoey, Garlicky Egg Scramble 201–2
  Courgette Flower Fritters with Ricotta, Lemon and Pistachios 25–7
  Fried Pizza Pockets and Fried Pizza Dough Sandwiches 221–3
  Lia's Mozzarella and Mint Rolls 205–6
  Little Pork, Pancetta and Cheese Parcels 61–2
  Little Puff Pies with Mozzarella and Tomato 229–30
  mozzarella 203–4
  Mozzarella-stuffed Meatloaf 63–5
  Oriel's Fig, Ricotta and Pistachio Salad 292–3
  Parsley and Mint Frittata 49–50
  Pasta Gratin with Meatballs 170–2
  ricotta 210–11
  Tagiolini with Wild Asparagus, Mascarpone and Lemon 188–9
cheesecake: Baked Ricotta and Pomegranate Cheesecake 212–13
cherries 243–4
  Cherry Jam 245–6
  Little Custard Cream Pies 236–8
  No-cook Cherries in Grappa 248
  Preserved Cherries in Syrup 247
chicken 70–2, 76

My Spatchcocked Chicken with Lemon, Garlic and Black Olives 77–9
Stitched-up Arse Chicken 73–5
chickpeas: Salento Chickpeas and Pasta 181–3
chillies 18
Mex-Italian Grilled Octopus 105–7
Stitched-up Arse Chicken 73–5
chipotle basil mayonnaise 105–7
chocolate: Chocolate and Almond Bites 285
Chocolate Olive Oil Mousse 157–8
Dark Chocolate and Hazelnut Cake 299–300
Little Custard Cream Pies 238
Chokoshvili, Lia 205
ciambiotto 88–90
ciceri e tria 181–3
cicoria 15
Bean Purée with Bitter Greens 51–2
ciliegie sciroppate 247
ciliegie sotto spirito 248
cime di rapa 15
Orecchiette with Bitter Greens 165–6
le cipolle al forno di Olivia 40–1
Cisternino 5, 198
citrus fruit 242
Candied Peel 265–6
clingfilm 10
cod: Salt Cod, Potato and Rice Gratin 108–10
coffee: *caffè nocciola* 296
Frozen Coffee and Cream 224–5
Iced Almond Milk Coffee 290
confettura di fichi, arancia e vino rosso 251–2
conversion charts 310–12
Courgette Flower Fritters with Ricotta, Lemon and Pistachios 25–7
Covid 7, 14, 120, 203, 218
cows 197
cozze arraganate 91–3
crema fredda al caffè 224–5
crema pasticcera 236–8
la cupeta 286–7
Custard Cream Pies 236–8
cuttlefish: fish stew 88–90

digestivi 260
dolcetti di pistacchi 294–5

eggs 8
Bread and Cheese Fritters 198–9
Cheesey, Tomatoey, Garlicky Egg Scramble 201–2
chipotle basil mayonnaise 105–7
Chocolate Olive Oil Mousse 157–8
Little Custard Cream Pies 236–8
Oven-cooked Agretti Frittata 47–8
Parsley and Mint Frittata 49–50
Pasta with Peas and Fried Eggs 184–5
Wild/Sprue Asparagus Frittata 45–6

fagiolini serpente 15
fave e cicoria 51–2
fennel: My Mother's Baked Fennel 53–4
Octopus, Fennel and Orange Salad 100
Ferragosto 170
fichi maritati 255
figs 249–50, 255–6, 279
Caramelised Fig Syrup 253–4
Fig, Orange and Red Wine Jam 251–2
Married Figs 255
Oriel's Fig, Ricotta and Pistachio Salad 292–3
il finocchio al forno di mia mamma 53–4
fish and seafood: Artichoke and Prawn Salad 38–9
Fish in Crazy Water 113–14
fish stew 86–90
Fried Pizza Pockets and Fried Pizza Dough Sandwiches 221–3
Mex-Italian Grilled Octopus 105–7
octopus 95–9
Octopus, Fennel and Orange Salad 100
Pugliese Octopus Salad 101
raw 94–5
Salt Cod, Potato and Rice Gratin 108–10
Saucier Braised Octopus 104
Seared Tuna and Rocket Salad 111–12
Slow-braised Octopus 102–3
Spaghetti with Prawns and Lemon 190–1
focaccia 124–5
focaccia barese 126–7
Potato and Rosemary Focaccia 128–30
focaccia con patate e rosmarino 128–30
Foggia 108
tiella foggiana 108–10
football 76
friggitelli al pomodoro 32–3
frise al pomodoro 231–2
frittata: Oven-cooked Agretti Frittata 47–8
Parsley and Mint Frittata 49–50
Wild/Sprue Asparagus Frittata 45–6
frittata d'agretti, al forno 47–8
frittata di asparagi selvatici 45–6
frittata di prezzemolo e menta 49–50

frittele di fiori di zucchina ripiene 25–7
fritters: Artichoke Fritters 36–7
Bread, Cheese and Aubergine Fritters 200
Bread and Cheese Fritters 198–9
Cavatelli Pasta with Bread Fritters and Aubergine in Tomato Sauce 167–9
Courgette Flower Fritters with Ricotta, Lemon and Pistachios 25–7
Fritter Puffs 233–5

Gallipoli 85, 133, 146, 148
Gallone, Pasquale 249
garlic: Cheesey, Tomatoey, Garlicky Egg Scramble 201–2
My Spatchcocked Chicken with Lemon, Garlic and Black Olives 77–9
granita di limone 226–7
grano arso 6, 163–4
grappa: No-cook Cherries in Grappa 248
Grigson, Jane 253, 292
My Mother's Baked Fennel 53–4
Sweetmeat Cake 269–70

ham: Pasta Gratin with Meatballs 170–2
hazelnuts 296
Dark Chocolate and Hazelnut Cake 299–300
Hazelnut Pesto 297–8
Sweetmeat Cake 269–70
herbs 17
see also individual herbs

ice cream: Persimmon Ice Cream 263
insalata di polpo al finocchio e arancia 100
Italy: diet 161–2

jam: sterilising jars 246
Cherry Jam 245–6
Fig, Orange and Red Wine Jam 251–2
Little Custard Cream Pies 238

lamb: Lemony Lamb Stew with Peas 68–69
lampascioni 6, 15–16
latte di mandorle 288–9
Lawrence, D. H. 255–6
Lecce: *caffè leccese* 290
Little Custard Cream Pies 5, 236–8
lemons 242
Almond Lemon Brittle 286–7
Candied Peel 265–6
Courgette Flower Fritters with Ricotta, Lemon and Pistachios 25–7
Icy Lemon Slush 226–7
Lemony Lamb Stew with Peas 68–9
Sicilian Lemon Peel Salad 264
Spaghetti with Prawns and Lemon 190–1
My Spatchcocked Chicken with Lemon, Garlic and Black Olives 77–9
Tagiolini with Wild Asparagus, Mascarpone and Lemon 188–9
lentils: Pasta and Lentils 179–80

maccheroncini 163
Pasta Gratin with Meatballs 170–2
Magna Graecia 85, 133
mandorle atterrate 285
Manduria 173
marmelatta di ciliegie 245–6
Martina Franca 28
mascarpone: Tagiolini with Wild Asparagus, Mascarpone and Lemon 188–9
mayonnaise: chipotle basil mayonnaise 105–7
meatballs 59–60
Orecchiette with Red Wine and Meatballs 173–4
Pasta Gratin with Meatballs 170–2
meatloaf: Mozzarella-stuffed Meatloaf 63–5
melanzane sott'olio 152–3
Mex-Italian Grilled Octopus 105–7
mince pies 271–2
mincemeat: Italian Spotted Dog 141
Italianish Orange and Walnut Mincemeat 267–8
mint 8
Lia's Mozzarella and Mint Rolls 205–6
Parsley and Mint Frittata 49–50
monks' beard *see agretti*
mortadella: Mozzarella-stuffed Meatloaf 63–5
Pasta Gratin with Meatballs 170–2
mousse: Chocolate Olive Oil Mousse 157–8
mozzarella 203–4
Cheesey, Tomatoey, Garlicky Egg Scramble 201–2
Fried Pizza Pockets and Fried Pizza Dough Sandwiches 221–3
Lia's Mozzarella and Mint Rolls 205–6
Little Puff Pies with Mozzarella and Tomato 229–30

Mozzarella-stuffed Meatloaf 63–5
Pasta Gratin with Meatballs 170–2
mozzarella water 140
Italian Spotted Dog 141
mushrooms: Cavatelli with King Oyster Mushrooms and Matchstick Potatoes 186–7
mussels: fish stew 88–90
Taranto-style Gratinated Mussels 91–3

nectarines: grilled nectarines 273–4
nocciola 296
Norman, Russell 3

octopus 95–9
cooking options 98–9
preparing 97
Mex-Italian Grilled Octopus 105–7
Octopus, Fennel and Orange Salad 100
Pugliese Octopus Salad 101
Saucier Braised Octopus 104
Slow-braised Octopus 102–3
olive dolci fritte ai peperoni 150
olive dolci fritti al pomodoro 149–50
olive oil 8, 147–8, 151
Aubergine Pickles 152–3
Chocolate Olive Oil Mousse 157–8
Hazelnut Pesto 297–8
Raw Pepper Pipone 156
Red Pepper Olive Oil Pickles 154–5
olives 8, 145–8
Craggy Tomato and Olive Rolls 137–9
Fried Sweet Olives with Red Peppers 150
Fried Sweet Olives with Tomato 149–50
Fritter Puffs 234–5
My Spatchcocked Chicken with Lemon, Garlic and Black Olives 77–9
Sweet-sour Aubergine with Tomato, Olives and Capers 21–2
onions: Caramelised Onion Pie 131–2
Olivia's roast onions 40–1
oranges 242, 243
Candied Peel 265–6
Fig, Orange and Red Wine Jam 251–2
Fritter Puffs 234
Italianish Orange and Walnut Mincemeat 267–8
Octopus, Fennel and Orange Salad 100
Orange and Almond Cake 273–4
orecchiette 162
Orecchiette with Bitter Greens 165–6
Orecchiette with Red Wine and Meatballs 173–4
orecchiette al Primitivo di Manduria 173–4
orecchiette alle cime di rapa 165–6
oregano 8
focaccia barese 126–7
Oria 5
Ostuni 4, 70, 151
Otranto 85
oven temperatures 312

pancetta: Little Pork, Pancetta and Cheese Parcels 61–2
pane di Altamura 119–20
panzerotti 221–3
panzerottini 223
parsley 8, 17
Parsley and Mint Frittata 49–50
Pasolini, Pier Paolo 210
passeggiata 217–18, 228
pasta 162–4
and beans 178
Cavatelli with King Oyster Mushrooms and Matchstick Potatoes 186–7
Cavatelli Pasta with Bread Fritters and Aubergine in Tomato Sauce 167–9
Orecchiette with Bitter Greens 165–6
Orecchiette with Red Wine and Meatballs 173–4
Pasta Gratin with Meatballs 170–2
Pasta and Lentils 179–80
Pasta with Peas and Fried Eggs 184–5
Salento Chickpeas and Pasta 181–3
Slow-cooked Beef or Veal Rolls in Tomato Sauce 175–7
Spaghetti with Prawns and Lemon 190–1
Tagiolini with Wild Asparagus, Mascarpone and Lemon 188–9
pasta al forno di Ferragosto 170–2
pasta e lenticchie 179–80
pasta e piselli 184–5
pasticciotti 236–8
peaches: Burrata with Peach and Almond Salad 209
peas: Lemony Lamb Stew with Peas 68–9
Pasta with Peas and Fried Eggs 184–5
peperonata 28–9
peperoni alla mollica 30
peppers 28
Fried Sweet Olives with Red Peppers 150

Friggitelli Peppers with Tomato 32–3
Puglian Fried Peppers with Breadcrumbs and Capers 30–1
Raw Pepper Pipone 156
Red Pepper Olive Oil Pickles 154–5
Sautéd Mess of Peppers 29
persimmons 262
Persimmon Sorbet or Ice Cream 263
Pescara 76
pesce all'acqua pazza 113–14
pesto: Hazelnut Pesto 297–8
pickles: Aubergine Pickles 152–3
Raw Pepper Pipone 156
Red Pepper Olive Oil Pickles 154–5
water processing 156
pies: Caramelised Onion Pie 131–2
Little Puff Pies with Mozzarella and Tomato 229–30
pignata di manzo 66–7
pipone 154–6
pistachios 291
Courgette Flower Fritters with Ricotta, Lemon and Pistachios 25–7
Oriel's Fig, Ricotta and Pistachio Salad 292–3
Soft Almond and Pistachio Biscuits 294–5
pitta di cipolle 131–2
pittule 233–5
pizzas: Fried Pizza Pockets and Fried Pizza Dough Sandwiches 221–3
pizzi leccesi 137–9
'Lu Pollu Cusutu N'Culu' 71–2
polpette di carne 59–60
polpette di melanzane 200
polpette di pane 198–9
Cavatelli Pasta with Bread Fritters and Aubergine in Tomato Sauce 167–9
polpettone ripieno 63–5
polpo alla pignata 102–3
pomegranate: Baked Ricotta and Pomegranate Cheesecake 212–13
Quince and Pomegranate Leather 257–9
pomelo: Candied Peel 265–6
pork: Little Pork, Pancetta and Cheese Parcels 61–2
Meatballs 59–60
Pork and Red Wine Stew 66–7
Porto Cesareo 5
potatoes: Cavatelli with King Oyster Mushrooms and Matchstick Potatoes 186–7
Pork and Red Wine Stew 66–7
Potato and Rosemary Focaccia 128–30
Pugliese Octopus Salad 101
Salt Cod, Potato and Rice Gratin 108–10
prawns 94
Artichoke and Prawn Salad 38–9
Spaghetti with Prawns and Lemon 190–1
Primitivo 173
pucce 133–6
pizzi leccesi 137–9
Puglia 3–6, 8
almonds 277–80
artichokes 34
bread 117–20
burrata 207
capers 18–19
caponata 19–20
cheese 195–6
cherries 243–4
chillies 18
citrus fruit 242–3
coast 83–5
Covid 7
cows 197
figs 249–50
fish stews 86
olives 145–8
pasta 162–3
peppers 28
raw fish and seafood 94–5
tomatoes 16–17
vegetables 14–16
wine 173
see also Ceglie Messapica
purple sprouting broccoli: Orecchiette with Bitter Greens 165–6

Quince and Pomegranate Leather 257–9
Quo Vado 71

raisins: Squash Caponata with Raisins and Toasted Almonds 23–4
rice: Salt Cod, Potato and Rice Gratin 108–10
ricotta 210–11
Baked Ricotta and Pomegranate Cheesecake 212–13
Courgette Flower Fritters with Ricotta, Lemon and Pistachios 25–7
Oriel's Fig, Ricotta and Pistachio Salad 292–3
La Ricotta (film) 210
Rocco, San 203

rocket: Burrata with Peach and Almond Salad 209
Seared Tuna and Rocket Salad 111–12
Roden, Claudia 273
rosata di mandorle 281–2
rosemary: Potato and Rosemary Focaccia 128–30
rustici leccesi 229–30

salads: Artichoke and Prawn Salad 38–9
Burrata with Peach and Almond Salad 209
Octopus, Fennel and Orange Salad 100
Oriel's Fig, Ricotta and Pistachio Salad 292–3
Pugliese Octopus Salad 101
Seared Tuna and Rocket Salad 111–12
Sicilian Lemon Peel Salad 264
Salento Chickpeas and Pasta 181–3
Salt Cod, Potato and Rice Gratin 108–10
San Giovanni Rotondo 84
scamorza: Fried Pizza Pockets and Fried Pizza Dough Sandwiches 221–3
Mozzarella-stuffed Meatloaf 63–5
sea bream: Fish in Crazy Water 113–14
semolina flour 121
Altamura-style Bread 122–3
'Crumbless' Flattish Sandwich Breads 135–6
focaccia barese 126–7
Sicilian Lemon Peel Salad 264
Siena 124
sorbet: Persimmon Sorbet 263
spaghetti ai gamberi e limone 190–1
Spaghetti with Prawns and Lemon 190–1
spinach: Bean Purée with Bitter Greens 51–2
spremuta 243
squash *see* butternut squash
squid: fish stew 88–90
Sweetmeat Cake 269–70

Tagiolini with Wild Asparagus, Mascarpone and Lemon 188–9
tagliata di tonno 111–12
taralli 219
Oriel's Fig, Ricotta and Pistachio Salad 292–3
Taranto 85, 91
tarts: Sweetmeat Cake 269–70
thyme: grilled nectarines 273–4
tiella foggiana 108–10
tomatoes 16–17
Cavatelli Pasta with Bread Fritters and Aubergine in Tomato Sauce 167–9
Cheesey, Tomatoey, Garlicky Egg Scramble 201–2
Craggy Tomato and Olive Rolls 137–9
Fried Pizza Pockets and Fried Pizza Dough Sandwiches 221–3
Fried Sweet Olives with Tomato 149–50
Friggitelli Peppers with Tomato 32–3
frise al pomodoro 231–2
Fritter Puffs 234–5
Little Puff Pies with Mozzarella and Tomato 229–30
Saucier Braised Octopus 104
Sautéd Mess of Peppers 29
Slow-cooked Beef or Veal Rolls in Tomato Sauce 175–7
Sweet-sour Aubergine with Tomato, Olives and Capers 21–2
torta di cioccolatto e nocciole 299–300
torta di ricotta e melograno al forno 212–13
Trani 84
tuna: Fried Pizza Pockets and Fried Pizza Dough Sandwiches 221–3
Seared Tuna and Rocket Salad 111–12
Turi 243–4

uova strapazzate al pomodoro e formaggio 201–2

veal: Meatballs 59–60
Slow-cooked Beef or Veal Rolls in Tomato Sauce 175–7
Vieste 4
vincotto di fichi 253–4
grilled nectarines 273–4

walnuts: Italianish Orange and Walnut Mincemeat 267–8
wine: Fig, Orange and Red Wine Jam 251–2
Orecchiette with Red Wine and Meatballs 173–4
Pork and Red Wine Stew 66–7

Xyllella fastidiosa 146–7

Zalone, Checco 71

CONVERSION CHARTS

Weight conversions

25/30g	1oz
40g	1½oz
50g	1¾oz
55g	2oz
70g	2½oz
85g	3oz
100g	3½oz
115g	4oz
150g	5½oz
200g	7oz
225g	8oz
250g	9oz
300g	10½oz
350g	12oz
375g	13oz
400g	14oz
450g	1lb
500g	1lb 2oz
600g	1lb 5oz
750g	1lb 10oz
900g	2lb
1kg	2lb 4oz
2kg	4lb 8oz

Volume conversions (liquids)

5ml	–	1 tsp
15ml	½fl oz	1 tbsp
30ml	1fl oz	2 tbsp
60ml	2fl oz	¼ cup
75ml	2½fl oz	⅓ cup
120ml	4fl oz	½ cup
150ml	5fl oz	⅔ cup
175ml	6fl oz	¾ cup
225ml	8fl oz	1 cup
350ml	12fl oz	1½ cups
500ml	18fl oz	2 cups
1 litre	1¾ pints	4 cups

Volume conversions (dry ingredients – an approximate guide)

Flour	125g	1 cup
Butter	225g	1 cup (2 sticks)
Breadcrumbs (dried)	125g	1 cup
Nuts	125g	1 cup
Seeds	160g	1 cup
Dried fruit	150g	1 cup
Dried pulses (large)	175g	1 cup
Grains & small pulses	200g	1 cup
Sugar	200g	1 cup

Oven temperatures

°C	°C with fan	°F	gas mark
110°C	90°C	225°F	¼
120°C	100°C	250°F	½
140°C	120°C	275°F	1
150°C	130°C	300°F	2
160°C	140°C	325°F	3
180°C	160°C	350°F	4
190°C	170°C	375°F	5
200°C	180°C	400°F	6
220°C	200°C	425°F	7
230°C	210°C	450°F	8
240°C	220°C	475°F	9

Length

5mm	¼ inch
1cm	½ inch
2cm	¾ inch
2.5cm	1 inch
3cm	1¼ inches
5cm	2 inches
8cm	3¼ inches
10cm	4 inches
15cm	6 inches
20cm	8 inches
23cm	9 inches
25cm	10 inches
28cm	11 inches
30cm	12 inches
35cm	14 inches